Obtaining Value from Big Data for Service Systems, Volume I

Obtaining Value from Big Data for Service Systems, Volume I

Big Data Management

Second Edition

Stephen H. Kaisler
Frank Armour
J. Alberto Espinosa
William H. Money

BEP BUSINESS EXPERT PRESS

Obtaining Value from Big Data for Service Systems, Second Edition,
Volume-I: Big Data Management
Copyright © Business Expert Press, LLC, 2019.

First published in 2019 by
Business Expert Press, LLC
222 East 46th Street, New York, NY 10017
www.businessexpertpress.com

ISBN-13: 978-1-94944-355-4 (paperback)
ISBN-13: 978-1-94944-356-1 (e-book)

Business Expert Press Service Systems and Innovations in Business and Society Collection

Collection ISSN: 2326-2664 (print)
Collection ISSN: 2326-2699 (electronic)

Cover and interior design by S4Carlisle Publishing Services Private Ltd., Chennai, India

First edition: 2016
Second edition: 2019

10 9 8 7 6 5 4 3 2 1

Printed in the United States of America.

Dedication

I would like to dedicate this book to my wife, Chryl, who has encouraged me and supported me in its preparation.

—Stephen H. Kaisler

I would like to thank my wife, Delphine Clegg, for her support and encouragement in preparing this book.

—J. Alberto Espinosa

To my wife, Rose, my parents, my children, and my grandchild: you make everything beautiful.

—Frank Armour

To my wonderful wife, Libby, whose continuous support and strength allow me to devote more energy to research and writing, and to my daughter, Katy, whose enduring dedication and commitment have taught me how to successfully close a project.

—William H. Money

Abstract

Big data is an emerging phenomenon that has enormous implications and impacts upon business strategy, profitability, and process improvements. All service systems generate big data these days, especially human-centered service systems such as government (including cities), health care, education, retail, finance, and so on. It has been characterized as the collection, analysis, and use of data characterized by the five Vs: volume, velocity, variety, veracity, and value (of data). As the plethora of data sources grows from sensors, social media, and electronic transactions, new methods for collecting or acquiring, integrating, processing, analyzing, understanding, and visualizing data to provide actionable information and support integrated and timely senior and executive decision making are required. The discipline of applying analytic processes to find and combine new sources of data and extract hidden crucial decision-making information from the oceans of data is rapidly developing, but requires expertise to apply in ways that will yield useful, actionable results for service organizations. Many service-oriented organizations that are just beginning to invest in big data collection, storage, and analysis need to address the numerous issues and challenges that abound—technological, managerial, and legal. Other organizations that have begun to use new data tools and techniques must keep up with the rapidly changing and snowballing work in the field. This booklet will help middle, senior, and executive managers to understand what big data is: how to recognize, collect, process, and analyze it; how to store and manage it; how to obtain useful information from it; and how to assess its contribution to operational, tactical, and strategic decision making in service-oriented organizations.

Keywords

analytic science; big data; business analytics; business intelligence; data science; descriptive analytics; enterprise architecture; NoSQL; predictive analytics; service delivery; service-oriented architecture

Contents

Purpose

This booklet is directed at senior executives and managers who need to understand the basic principles of big data as it is used to support service delivery, the tools and technology to develop and implement a big data support group within one's own organization, the roles and skills of personnel who will comprise such a group, and some of the challenges they will face in deploying and operating such an organization.

Acknowledgments

First, we would like to thank Haluk Demirkan for providing us with the opportunity to prepare this book and Jim Spohrer for his encouragement in seeing it to completion. We would also like to thank Haluk and Christer Carlsson for the opportunity to organize a big data minitrack and to provide encouragement and support for our tutorials on Big Data and Advanced Analytics at the 46th through 49th Hawaii International Conferences on Systems Science (HICSS). We also thank the many paper presenters and attendees at our minitracks and tutorials who have provided many insights and cogent comments on big data and analytics.

List of Acronyms

ACO	Accountable Care Organization
AnBoK	Analytics Body of Knowledge
ANOVA	Analysis of Variance
API	Application Programming Interface
APT	Advanced Persistent Threats
B2B	Business-to-Business
BDA	Big Data Analytics
BI	Business Intelligence
CAO	Chief Analytics Officer
CAP	Certified Analytics Professional
CDO	Chief Data Officer
CHIP	Children's Health Insurance Program
CIFS	Common Internet File System
CMM	Capability Maturity Model
CMMS	Centers for Medicare and Medicaid Services
CSV	Comma Separated Values
DARPA	Defense Advanced Research Projects Agency
DB	Data Base
DBMS	Data Base Management System
EA	Enterprise Architecture
ETL	Extract, Transform, Load
FEAF	Federal Enterprise Architecture Framework
GPU	Graphics Processing Unit

HHS	Health and Human Services
HPC	High Performance Computing
HTML	HyperText Markup Language
IBM	International Business Machines Corporation
IDC	International Data Corporation
IDE	Interactive Development Environment
IDS	Intrusion Detection System
INFORMS	Institute for Operations Research and Management Sciences
IoT	Internet of Things
IPv6	Internet protocol, version 6
IT	Information Technology
LAMP	Linux-Apache-MySQL-Perl/PHP/Python
LEAP	Linux-Eucalyptus-AppScale-Python
MAMP	MacOS-Apache-MySQL-Perl/PHP/Python
MOOC	Massive Open Online Course
MPI	Message Passing Interface
NAP	National Academies Press
NFL	National Football League
NFS	Network File System
NIST	National Institute of Science and Technology
NLP	Natural Language Processing
NSF	National Science Foundation
OLAP	OnLine Analytical Processing
OMB	Office of Management and Budget
OODA	Observe, Orient, Decide, Act
OSGI	Open Source Gateway Initiative
OSS	Open Source Software
PhD	Doctor of Philosophy

RDBMS	Relational Data Base Management System
RETMA	Radio Electronics Television Manufacturers Association
RFID	Radio Frequency Identification
RTBDA	Real-Time Big Data Analytics
SDM	Service Delivery Model
SLA	Service Level Agreement
SOA	Service-Oriented Architecture
SOC	Security Operations Center
SSN	Social Security Number
STEM	Science, Technology, Engineering and Mathematics
TOGAF	The Open Group Architectural Framework
UPC	Universal Product Code
VPN	Virtual Private Network
WAMP	WindowsOS-Apache-MySQL-Perl/PHP/Python
WEKA	Waikato Environment for Knowledge Analysis
WSJ	Wall Street Journal
XML	eXtended Markup Language
ZB	Zettabytes

CHAPTER 1

Introduction

The Internet, the World Wide Web, and the concept of service delivery have revolutionized the way commercial, academic, governmental, and nongovernmental organizations deal with their suppliers and their clients and customers. Individuals and organizations are overwhelmed with data produced by IT systems that are so pervasive throughout society, government, and business. The wide variety and huge numbers of data sources, including sensors, cell phones, tablets, and other devices, are increasing at a seemingly exponential rate. Estimates (2010) were that all sources of data, including replicated data such as retweets and resends of e-mail, amount to tens of exabytes per month, that is, 10^{18} or 1,000,000,000,000,000,000 bytes. The numbers are staggering, and, obviously, no one knows for sure. In 2012, the International Data Corporation (IDC) estimated the volume of data at 2.8 zettabytes (ZB) and forecasted that we would generate 40 ZB by 2020 (http://www .webopedia.com/quick_ref/just-how-much-data-is-out-there.html). Our data generation is growing exponentially.

Individuals and organizations do not actively collect, own, process, or analyze this much data themselves. However, many individuals and organizations acquire and deal with gigabytes of data, and many organizations utilize terabytes and petabytes of data per year. Senior executives and managers in government, academia, and business operations are grappling with the deluge of data available to them and are trying to make decisions and conclusions based on it. A critical area is how to collect, organize, process, store, and analyze this flood of data in order to deliver superior services to their clients and customer base—both internal and external.

Much of this data is generated from the services sector of the economy: health, manufacturing, marketing, telecommunications, and so on. To address this wealth of data and the underlying technology and practices, IBM pioneered the use of the term *service science* to encompass the broad spectrum of business, teaching, and research expertise required to develop the capabilities to sustain and advance the services environment that we live in today. Advances in technology have made large volumes of data available to users and providers within the services environment. This volume of data has come to be called big data and has its own business, teaching, and research expertise associated with it.

In this book we describe how coordinating and integrating the expertise between the services environment and the big data environment has led and is continuing to lead to enhanced service delivery to customers and clients and to increased revenues and profits in many industries. However, despite the attention given to it in the popular press and the blogosphere, many more opportunities exist and even more will be invented so that more organizations can derive benefits and value from the analysis of big data.

Defining Big Data

There are many definitions of big data. Our preferred definition, cited in Kaisler, Armour, Espinosa, and Money (2013), is as follows: *Big data is the volume of data that cannot be efficiently organized and processed with the storage and tools that we currently possess.* Under certain circumstances, we can organize, process, and analyze big data. However, we cannot do it very efficiently or effectively. For example, because we cannot process a real-time data stream fast enough, we cannot generate results that will enable decision-making within a specified observe, orient, decide, and act (OODA) cycle.

While big data often implies many very large volumes of data, it can also, as Leslie Johnston (2013) noted, "most definitely mean small data files but a lot of them." These extremes present challenges to business and IT managers and owners on a daily basis.

How do you know when you are facing big data? Well, the transition from organizational data and databases to big data is not exact, but there are a number of characteristics that can be used to help one understand when the transition occurs. The initial three Vs were first stated by Doug Laney (2001). Big data has been characterized by several attributes. We have defined the five Vs as described in Table 1.1 (Kaisler et al. 2013). Based on our research and experience, we have added the last two Vs. Other definitions for the Vs abound, but we consider these to be the primary five definitions.

Table 1.1 Five Vs of big data

V	Description
Data volume	*Data volume* measures the amount of data collected by and available to an organization, which does not necessarily have to own all of it as long as it can access it. As data volume increases, the value of different data records will decrease in proportion to age, type, richness, and quantity, among other factors. It is estimated that over 2.5 exabytes (10^{18}) of data is created every day, as of 2012 (Wikipedia 2013).
Data velocity	*Data velocity* measures the speed of data streaming, its aggregation, and its accumulation. Data velocity also has connotations of how quickly it gets purged, how frequently it changes, and how fast it becomes outdated. E-commerce has rapidly increased the speed and richness of data used for different business transactions (e.g., website clicks). Data velocity management is much more than a bandwidth issue; it is also an ingest issue (the extract-transform-load [ETL] problem).
Data variety	*Data variety* is a measure of the richness of the data representation—either *structured*, such as resource description framework (RDF) files, databases, and Excel tables, or *unstructured*, such as text, audio files, and video. From an analytic perspective, it is probably the biggest obstacle to effectively using large volumes of data. Incompatible data formats, nonaligned data structures, and inconsistent data semantics represent significant challenges that can lead to analytic sprawl.
Data value	*Data value* measures the usefulness of data in making decisions. It has been noted that "the purpose of computing is insight, not numbers." Data science is exploratory and useful in getting to know the data, but "analytic science" encompasses the predictive power of big data. A large amount of data may be valueless if it is perishable, late, imprecise, or has other weaknesses or flaws.
Data veracity	*Data veracity* is the accuracy, precision, and reliability of the data. A data set may have very accurate data with low precision and low reliability based on the collection methods and tools or the data generation methods. The information and results generated by processing this data may then be seriously flawed or compromised.

Big data has often been used to represent a large volume of data of one type, such as text or numbers or pixels. Recently, many organizations are creating blended data from data sources with varied data types through analysis and processing. These data come from instruments, sensors, Internet transactions, e-mail, social media such as Twitter, YouTube, Reddit, Pinterest, Tumblr, RFID devices, and from clickstreams. New data types may be derived through analysis or by joining different types of data.

Getting Started with Big Data

Research and practical analysis have shown that there are many areas where you can focus your attention. We will review four process areas that are enormously fruitful for immediate analysis of processes using the tools that can best be applied to big data.

First, *data categorization* can aid in the analysis of big data, because the tools available now permit machine-learning algorithms to explore large and varied data collections through machines that are trained or seeded with previously known classifications, such as process output or groupings. The value of these groupings is that they will provide classifications or labeled analysis variables that may then be used to discover a relationship or a predictor that shows or predicts the value or the output of the process. It may be the result of a hidden value that is a part within the process—input, subprocess, step, or activity—or a characteristic of the process input. This analysis is truly a directed discovery process and an organizational learning experience enabled by big data (Deng, Runger, and Tuv 2012; Hwang, Runger, and Tuv 2007). The data does not have to be fully classified or categorized because specific techniques can be applied to assign grouping or to cluster data or process outputs that do not appear within the previous groupings (Zhang et al. 2010). The value is that this categorization develops insights required to understand the root causes of underlying problems by discovering relations that were simply not previously visible. This process was used in cancer prediction, diagnosis, and in understanding its development (Cruz and Wishart 2006).

Secondly, *functional data analysis* can be implemented because it permits discrete calculations due to the continuous nature of production data (Ferraty and Romain 2011). This section will not attempt to describe this analysis in great detail, but the reader should be aware of the benefits of this form of big data analysis. This application analysis is closely related to profile monitoring and control charting that is employed when the quality of a process or product can be characterized by a functional relationship between a production measure of some output or output value and an explanatory variable(s). We can often "see" these relationships (but may not fully understand the value) in the graphs, curves, and visual depictions prepared when data are logged and drawn as graphs or curves. The business value is obvious in being able to predict strength and changes, and in locating when relationships may begin and end.

The value of this can be recognized in the potential for assessing quality characteristics such as size and quantity data, product shapes, geometric relationships, appearances of faults and imperfections, patterns, and surface finish, while these are happening, and relate them directly to end results of processes. Data may be produced by visual sensors, by image observation in many medical, military, and scientific applications, or by other mechanisms (Megahed, Woodall, and Camelio 2011).

Third, managers must now recognize that situations that can be "drawn" as graphs showing associations between various objects in the data can be analyzed as big data problems. Graphic representations (Cook and Holder 2006) are seen as two connected nodes with an edge, if the nodes possess a relationship. Researchers have used these data to assess social networks (e.g., Facebook, LinkedIn), intrusions for networks, disease, or product adoption, and rating or rankings for consumer e-commerce actions (Chakrabarti and Faloutsos 2012). For example, one can identify potential changes in social network data sets or communications networks. McCulloh et al. (2008) found variances in the Al-Qaeda network prior to September 11. For the business, it could be important to know that sources of data and information acquisition are changing for clients or business customers.

Finally, in the era of big data, data may now be available simultaneously from numerous and unrelated sources. Historically, a control chart was employed to observe multiple sources of periodic data (Boyd 1950). Automated tests can now be used to detect the likelihood of changes in only one stream of data and concurrently monitoring multiple streams based on the stream features, assessing correlations among the streams, and the scope and size of any change sought (Jirasettapong and Rojanarowan 2011).

Adding Value to Organizations

Big data has an impact in every field of human endeavor, if the data is available and can be processed. Impact is different from value. Impact helps to advance a field with new knowledge whereas value affects how useful the resulting actionable information is—whether predicting events, making a profit, discovering a new particle, or improving the lot of our fellow humans. Big data can add value in several ways: (1) It can make information transparent and usable at a higher frequency. (2) As more accurate data is collected, it allows organizations to conduct more controlled experiments to assess efficiency and refine business operations. (3) It can focus attention on narrower segments of the customer community for precisely specifying products and services (market segmentation). (4) Given usage data, it can be used for the specification of new products and services.

In a research study by IBM and the Said Business School, Oxford University (Turner, Schroeck, and Shockley 2012), four areas for employing big data were identified as described in Table 1.2.

Note the use of the word "analytics" throughout this book. Analytics are essential to deriving insights, new data and value from big data. Analytics allow business leaders to process large quantities of data to obtain a robust image of what's going on in their organization.

Outline of This Book

In this Second Edition, the original volume has been divided into two volumes: Volume I comprising chapters 1, 2, 3 and 5 from the original volume, and Volume II comprising chapters 4, 6, and 7 from the original volume.

This chapter has provided a brief introduction to some of the issues and challenges that senior executives and managers must consider in using big data to assess and enhance their service delivery operations.

Table 1.2 Areas for use of big data

Using big data	Brief description
Customer analytics	IBM and Said noted that 55% of the companies they surveyed focus their big data efforts on customer-centered objectives in order to improve service delivery to their diverse customer base. These companies want to improve their ability to anticipate varying market conditions and customer preferences in order to take advantage of market opportunities to improve customer service and increase customer loyalty in an agile manner.
Build upon scalable and extensible information foundation	IBM and Said noted that companies believe results can be obtained from big data only if the IT and information infrastructure can respond to evolving aspects of big data focused on the three Vs: variety, velocity, and volume. This means they must be able to evolve their IT and information infrastructure in an agile manner, transparently to customer interactions. (Note: They only examined the original three Vs, but we believe that the information foundation must be focused on the five Vs.)
Initial focus is on gaining insights from existing and new sources of big data	IBM and Said found that most initial big data efforts are focused on analyzing existing data sets and stores in order to have a near-term effect on business operations. They suggest that this is a pragmatic approach to beginning to develop a big data usage capability. Most companies do not know what insights they will gain or how much useful and usable information they can extract from the information on hand. In many cases, the data has been collected, perhaps organized, and stored away for many years without ever being analyzed.
Requires strong analytics	Using big data requires a variety of analytics tools and the skills to use them. Typically, companies use such tools as data mining, online analytical processing (OLAP), statistical packages, and the like on structured data based on existing data stores, marts, and warehouses. However, as they accumulate unstructured data, the diversity of data types and structures requires new techniques for analysis and visualization. Existing tools can have trouble scaling to the volumes characteristic of big data and, often, cannot adequately analyze geospatial data, voice, video, or streaming data.

The remaining chapters provide additional information on each of the major topics presented earlier and present a framework for gaining value from this growing phenomenon.

The remainder of this book is divided into three chapters as follows:

- *Chapter 2: Applications of Big Data to Service Delivery* will discuss how big data can be used within the service delivery paradigm to deliver better quality of service and to identify and target a larger universe of potential customers.
- *Chapter 3: Analyzing Big Data for Successful Results* explains the types of analytics that may be applied to big data to yield actionable information and also identifies different analytical packages.
- *Chapter 5: Building an Effective Big Data Organization* discusses the organizational structure of a big data operation, how to staff it, and the key characteristics of the staff.
- This volume has focused on the management aspects of big data, whereas Volume II focuses on the technological aspects.

CHAPTER 2

Applications of Big Data to Service Delivery

Organizations can, and are, utilizing big data to improve and enhance the delivery of services to their customers. From retail marketing to financial services to health care and more, big data and analytics are changing the landscape of service delivery. We first outline a simple, generic service delivery model (SDM) and then discuss how big data can be applied within the model. We then outline several examples of how big data is currently being applied to service delivery.

Defining Services

A *service* is often described as a tangible or intangible benefit provided by a person, a group, an organization, or some other entity to a person, a group, an organization, or some other entity. There are many types of services: providing advice as in the case of WebMD, providing education through Massive Open Online Courses (MOOCs), or selling airline tickets. In the latter case, the service is not the airline ticket itself, but the transaction(s) leading to the exchange of money for the airline ticket, whether physical or electronic. Thus, a service is differentiated from a "good" in that it is nonmaterial and does not incorporate a notion of ownership. In the example given earlier, the airline ticket, whether paper or electronic, is the "good" that is owned by the person purchasing it.

Whereas earlier services used to describe and document the exchange of information verbally or in written form between humans, today services are most often exchanged through e-mail, social media, and online systems such as Amazon, Google, Wikipedia, YouTube, Twitter, product ordering systems, and so on. A service is frequently manifested as the cocreation of value between the entities involved. For example, the purchase of airline tickets through Expedia, Travelocity, or Orbitz involves the exchange of items of value: electronic tickets, electronic payments via credit card or PayPal, a sense of accomplishment in completing a task, and a sense of anticipation in taking a trip.

Since definitions are often constraining, we will utilize a broad conceptualization of a service. In general, *if something provides value, and is almost or immediately usable—without modification and without understanding exactly how it functions—it is likely a service in the eyes of the purchaser.* Services can be modified by the delivering organization and are frequently enhanced and upgraded at the customer's request or to match the benefits provided by competitors. Such changes may not be particularly important to the client unless they cause an organization to change its operation, the client to pay more for using the service, or remove something the client deems to be of significance or value.

Using our loose, but applied, definition as a huge net, one may characterize many businesses and organizations as service businesses. For example, generally accepted services organizations include those in the financial, medical, education, government, utilities, and many other sectors.

As an example, consider the recent development of the Healthcare Marketplace. Many will agree that it meets the conditions established as being those of a service. It offers itself as a resource where you can learn about your health coverage options, compare health insurance plans based on costs, benefits, and other important features, choose a plan, and enroll in coverage. The marketplace establishes conditions for its service in that it delivers information on programs to low- and moderate-income individuals who may not have the resources to pay for coverage.

The service provided through this marketplace includes information that describes how users may save on the monthly premiums and save out-of-pocket costs of insurance coverage (available through the marketplace), as well as Medicaid information, and Children's Health Insurance Program (CHIP) data. The service is conditional and rules-based in that it may be managed by a state or by the Centers for Medicare and Medicaid Services (CMMS), which are a part of the Department of Health and

Human Services (HHS). Potential users may access HealthCare.gov, or if one lives in a state with its own exchange, one can be guided to their state's marketplace site. Conditions for the use of data are described, and conditions applying to the state sites are located on state exchanges. Finally, this service describes the use of information, sharing of data, questions, and user data that must be provided to obtain the service, requirements for identifying social security numbers (SSNs), rules about citizenship, outcome questions about end result determinations, and privacy rules (https://www.healthcare.gov/how-we-use-your-data/).

A second example in the financial services arena will illustrate the breadth and depth of the processes and business rules that govern the services provided in service industries and organizations. Financial services are products that deliver process management solutions that are both end results and stepping stones to process reengineering and technological change. Often, the services may result in reduced costs and enhanced operational performance for the customers of the service organizations. The services will implement portions of the business models of many organizations to control costs and support growth. The diverse range of available financial services includes those depicted in Table 2.1. The concept of big data in the finance arena can become very complex when the transactions are enumerated with such a laundry list.

Table 2.1 Financial services

leasing and lending	maintenance for client accounts and transactions	
asset tracking, management, and assessments	delinquency tracking	deal conversions
backroom operations	outsourcing	customer remediation
revenue accounting and profitability assessment	security originations and settlements	money transfers
reconciliation	mortgage origination	sales and marketing
closing and funding	post close/QC	customer collections
underwriting	social media	risk and fraud
card services	payments, lending, and deposits,	account setup and maintenance

Service Systems

A *service system* is a complex system in which specific arrangements of people, organizational networks, and technologies take actions that provide value for others. *Service delivery* is the set of mechanisms, including manual, semiautomated, and automated systems of hardware, software, and communications that convey a service from one entity to another. A *service-oriented architecture* (SOA) is the foundation of a service delivery system. Services are components that provide functionality to the other components in an application through a communication protocol over a network. The interfaces to services (e.g., the APIs) are published and described to facilitate access to the services.

A service system is a human-made system that provides value in provider–customer interactions. Providers and customers may be humans or computers, or both, as in semiautomatic systems. The advent of online systems meant that humans do not necessarily need to be "in the loop"; hence, the concept of service delivery as the exchange of electronic information between two computer systems, for example, in a *business-to-business* (B2B) service system.

Big Data in Service Delivery

Understanding the growing role of big data in service delivery requires that one appreciates the scope, value, and importance of service processes, and how big data has impacted many services. We will illustrate the growing importance of the role of processes and their growing impact in the service industry in this section.

Managers and executives reading this text may come from many different service industries, each with a growing set of processes that are important for the provided services. Each industry, business, and organization will have its own vision and firm understanding of what comprises the business model, processes, operations and services, and the outcomes or customer benefits, either objective or perceived, of what is provided to clients.

Key processing issues may be predetermined by the business operation plan of the organization. The organization generally has as its business objective the provision of a clear set of services for each customer.

Services may provide intangible results, such as information or electronic tickets, or tangible results, such as a package showing up on your doorstep. The proposed benefit may be more or less clear, and may need to be specified in greater detail as a component of any service transaction with the client. A customer benefiting from the service will have an expectation of what is to be received or gained from a service and the conditions that may be necessary for the benefit to be received.

Thus, the entire service can be viewed as a process, with one who purchases a service having a clear understanding of what is being gained, what the service accomplishes, and conversely what is not intended to be a result. The conditions may be explicit, in that limits, costs, dates, durations, guidance for the purchase, support, and even limits on the acquiring client may be explicitly stated. All of these may be determined by contracts, either explicitly stated or implied. The implications of this kind of task specificity are clear. The service organization will follow processes and procedures governed by business rules that ensure the delivery of the service if the processes and conditions are correctly followed—for example, on the business side, the actions required to provide the service to the user are well understood and correctly, consistently, and completely implemented.

A key idea in service delivery is that services are produced and consumed at the same time. Thus, the customer receives the ticket or some notification of it at the same time that money is provided to pay for it. What is produced and consumed here is the transaction that affects the exchange. However, consumption may be delayed in some services, as, for example, in parcel transportation and delivery, where the customer provides the package and the payment at one point in time, but the package is delivered some time later to its recipient, thus completing the service.

The goal of service delivery is to provide value, which means the exchange of information and, sometimes, objects that must be mutually beneficial to both or all parties to the set of interactions. In a service-oriented environment, the critical elements are: (1) service delivery being the focal point of customer interaction, (2) understanding the needs and requirements of the (possibly diverse) customer base, and (3) ensuring the privacy and security of customer interactions, whether human-to-business or business-to-business interactions.

Service science is the application of scientific methods to advance our ability to design, improve, and scale service systems for business, governmental, and societal purposes (Maglio and Spohrer 2008). Service systems are inherently dynamic, complex, and continually changing in modern society. Thus, there is no single type of service system, but many types, and more to emerge in the next several years as innovation in interactive, always-on technology advances and drives the evolution of service.

A Service Delivery Model

While there are a multitude of service delivery approaches, we broadly define a *service delivery model* (SDM) as a set of principles, policies, and processes used to guide the design, development, operation, and retirement of services delivered by a service provider with a view to offering a consistent service experience to a specific user community. Services are both inward- and outward-facing. Inward-facing services include support services and operations management services. Outward-facing services to the customer base include a variety of product, management, analytics, and professional services.

Figure 2.1 outlines a simplified SDM that we use to represent basic service delivery components. Many implemented SDMs can become complex and their description is beyond the scope of this book.

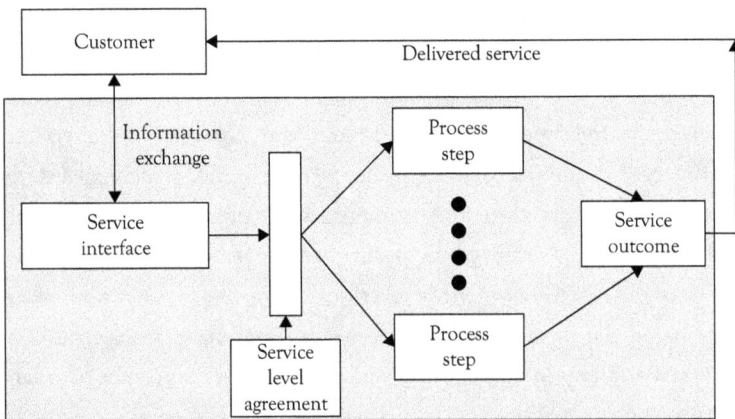

Figure 2.1 Simplified SDM

There are four key elements to service delivery (Service Futures 2019) as listed below:

1. Service culture: This is a set of critical principles according to which the management controls, maintains, and develops the social processes that manifest itself as delivery of service and gives value to customers.
2. Employee engagement: The best designed processes and systems will only be effective if carried out by people with higher engagement. Engagement is the moderator between the design and the execution of the service excellence model.
3. Service quality: Service processes must promote quality and be accompanied by systems and metrics to assess the service's quality by evaluating how well it helps customers to fulfill their mission.
4. Customer experience: This refers to a constant evaluation of how the customer perceives the service and the service provider's delivery as part of the collaborative effort to satisfy both parties.

Business customers are individuals, and the communities and markets they reside in provide the services for them to interact with each other. Depending on the number and makeup of customer groups, a service-based organization may segment them into different groups or communities. Customers interact with a *service interface*, exchanging information, perhaps through multiple exchanges (such as in transaction processing where one moves through multiple web pages). Each interaction may activate one or more steps to process the information and perform actions to satisfy the service. Ultimately, the service produces an outcome, such as an electronic ticket, a bill of lading, a shipping receipt, or a piece of information, which is returned to the customer.

Service management ensures that the organization is offering the right services at the right quality and price levels within its market. Typically, the services are described and managed in a *service portfolio* or catalog. The service management component is responsible for the life cycle management of services and their financial viability. *Service level agreements* (SLAs) can be used to guarantee performance-based service levels to the business customer.

Coupling Big Data to Service Delivery

Big data has the potential to improve service delivery in a wide variety of ways. For example, big data customer and market analytics can be used to identify customers for new or existing services based on current buying patterns, geography, income status, and so on.

More and more organizations are concerned about how their services are being characterized in social media, which can indicate, for example, the level of customer satisfaction. Social media review sites can be harvested and analyzed to determine how customers view the current service levels (e.g., excellent, good, fair, poor). Organizations utilize big data social media analytics to capture unstructured comments on blogs, review sites, media articles, and so on. They can perform reputational analysis on the data so that the service provider better understands how the quality of their services is perceived by their customers and utilizes that information to improve service delivery. Some examples include:

- For organizations such as telecom companies, the levels of network availability and bandwidth can be tracked in real time via big data.
- For package delivery, taxi, and other transportation-intense services, providers can utilize dynamic transportation and geolocation data to perform real-time tracking and issue alerts on current vehicle location, time to next appointment, current traffic patterns, and so on, helping to ensure performance-based SLAs.

Supporting Service Delivery with Big Data

As increasing amounts of data are generated and almost unlimited storage and computing capabilities become available (e.g., Clouds, HPC Clusters), big data has become the next major frontier in IT innovation. It offers unprecedented opportunities for discovering hidden intelligence and game-changing insights in business and other domains. By using data collected to support their users, but also by simultaneously collecting data from their users, large search companies such as Yahoo and Google have been able to derive deeper and better business insights than were previously available. The potential for generating new business value has led industry, academia, government, and commercial organizations to invest in *big data analytics* (BDA) in order to seek new business opportunities and to deliver new levels of services to their customers and clients.

Analytics is about extracting meaning out of data. *Business analytics* is a set of methods or procedures for analyzing an organization's data to elicit information that can help the organization improve its business operations and decisions. Today, business analytics are largely statistically based processes applied to data to drive decision making. Business analytics is about framing a business question, identifying data to answer that question, selecting appropriate models and predictors, and writing up the results and conclusions. Once a particular analytic approach has proven useful and similar questions recur, we enter the realm of *business intelligence*. Business intelligence is a suite of tools and techniques for transforming raw data into meaningful and useful information to support business operations. Among the tools and techniques in this suite are reporting, data mining, text mining, and predictive analytics. Table 2.2 describes different categories of analytics.

Table 2.2 Categories of analytics

Category	Description
Descriptive analytics	Looks at data and analyzes past events for insight to understand the nature of the data at hand. It is always the first step in any analytics project.
Diagnostic analytics	Uses data to determine why something happened, like for example, equipment failure, market downturns, etc.
Predictive analytics	Uses data to determine the probable outcome based on other data (i.e., predictors). There are many types of predictive analytics modeling approaches, but they are generally classified by outcome (i.e., quantitative vs. likelihood; for example, good vs. bad loan) or by method (i.e., regression vs. tree approaches).
Prescriptive analytics	Goes beyond predicting future outcomes by also suggesting actions to benefit from the predictions and/or how to avoid bad situations, and by showing the decision maker the implications of each decision option. This category of analytics draws heavily from decision sciences and operations research.
Decisive analytics	Goes beyond prescriptive analytics to operationally specify how to accomplish a goal or objective in some detail (akin to tactical and operational planning).
Visual analytics	Has emerged from scientific visualization to focus on analytical reasoning facilitated by interactive visual interfaces.

Organizations have been using analytics to assess performance and facilitate decision making since the first organizations were formed. Up until the beginning of the electronic calculator age, circa the 1900s, most analytic systems were manual, for example, human computers. Analytics received a strong boost from Frederick Taylor and Edward Deming, among others, in the early years of the twentieth century. Another strong proponent was Robert McNamara, while President and Chairman at Ford Motor Company, then at the Department of Defense. The advent of electronic computers, programming systems, and other tools moved analytics into the software arena.

Big data in a vacuum cannot ensure that any services will change or that there will be service delivery improvements. Big data must be analyzed within the context of a business, scientific, or any other type of system. The role of analytics is to transform, process, and display big data and the results from its analysis to users to enable them to solve specific and particular problems.

Data-Driven Companies

The International Data Corporation (IDC) suggests that companies that embrace big data are on track to being successful in this evolving era of big data. We provide some examples below.

Under Armour, a company based in Baltimore, MD, is a successful sportswear manufacturer that continually seeks to bring innovative changes to sportswear. For the National Football League (NFL), they embedded sensors in the shorts worn by NFL candidates at their tryouts to help evaluate the parameters of the play. John Deere and Co., famed for its farm equipment among other machines, changed to an agile model of software development. It can now deploy new software on a monthly basis directly to tractors every month or so that helps them drive straight across plowed fields.

The *Harvard Business Review* (McAfee and Brynjolfsson 2012) noted that companies using data-driven decision making are 5 percent more productive and 6 percent more profitable than their competitors. IDC noted that data-driven companies that use diverse data sources and diverse analytic methods are five times more likely to succeed in their projects than competitors that do not.

Retail Analytics

Walmart typically handles more than 1 million customer transactions every hour (2.5 petabytes of data) and utilizes analytics in most aspects of the sales and inventory processes.

However, analytics are not new for retailers, as they have been doing analysis of point-of-sale transactions and other business data for years. The first barcode data appeared in the 1970s. It was placed on a pack of Wrigley's chewing gum scanned via Universal Product Code (UPC) in the Marsh Supermarket, in Troy, OH, in 1974. It became the basis for tracking merchandise sales in supermarkets, which operated at a slim profit margin, and then expanded to many other stores. Today, UPC data is widely used and allows major retailers to track purchases by customers and predict their purchasing behavior.

Radio-frequency identification devices (RFIDs) are becoming ubiquitous and offer the ability to dynamically track items as they move. Similarly, with cellphones and Wi-Fi, many companies can now detect cellphones within close proximity to a store, office, or other facility and, knowing something about the owner, transmit targeted advertising to the cellphone.

Examples of retail BDA include:

- Customer analytics
- Merchandising analytics
- Store operations
- Marketing analytics
- Return, fraud, and loss prevention analytics

Health Care

Health systems, hospitals, Accountable Care Organizations (ACOs), and physicians are becoming increasingly concerned about how the quality of service they provide to their patients is perceived in the marketplace. An industry shift toward transparency and consumerism is giving patients-as-consumers access to an unprecedented and growing number of health care data sources to search for and evaluate health care providers, while the proliferation of social media is changing industry dynamics.

As patients-as-consumers flock to online media outlets such as rating/ review sites and social media channels to share their experiences, health care providers are now looking for better ways to monitor and analyze this feedback, as value-driven government and commercial payers tie reimbursements to quality assessments in which patient satisfaction data is a factor. Consequently, pay-for-performance is driving demand from health care organizations for more data, better collection methods, standardized metrics, and more robust analytics applications to better understand patient satisfaction to improve their quality of service.

Binary Fountain, a McLean, VA, company, is a provider of patient feedback management solutions uniquely designed for health care in a single cloud-based platform. Their proprietary healthcare-centric natural language processing engine mines patient feedback and commentary harvested from a growing number of public sources, then analyzes and benchmarks patient sentiment tied to 37 operational performance categories. This holistic approach to patient feedback management empowers operations, patient experience teams, and marketing and advertising executives with insights that drive improvements to operational decision making, resulting in reduced costs, strengthened brand positioning, higher revenues, better patient engagement, and better quality of services.

Fraud Detection

FICO Falcon, a credit card fraud detection system, protects 2.1 billion active accounts worldwide. It is a BDA tool for the early detection of fraudulent activity on credit and debit cards. This system predicts the probability of fraud on an account by comparing current transactions (e.g., normal cardholder activity) to current fraud trends.

It utilizes real-time, transaction-based scoring with neural network models, and provides real-time decision making on suspected fraudulent transactions. It has adaptive models that can adjust to changing patterns in cases of attempted fraud. The result is more secure and less costly credit card services to consumers, credit card providers, and the merchants that accept the cards.

Mass Transit

Bridj, a transit startup, has introduced a pop-up bus transportation system in Boston that adapts in real time to ridership needs. It uses a network of express shuttles that offer efficient and flexible trips that are dynamic, scheduled based on predictions of changing user transport. The system analyzes "between two and three billion data points to understand how Boston moves, from over 19 different data streams," including municipal data, census data, and social media data. It then targets neighborhoods it considers commuter pain points.

The system has cut some commute times in half by strategically offering bus services and routing in the city. For example, a ride from Coolidge Corner to Kendall Square, which would likely take 42 to 55 minutes on the Massachusetts Bay Transportation Authority buses, has taken 15 to 18 minutes on its buses.

CHAPTER 3

Analyzing Big Data for Successful Results

Some companies have built their very businesses on their ability to collect, analyse, and act on data.

—*Competing on Analytics* by Tom Davenport

Brad Peters (2014) has noted that the bloom of big data may be fading. Where it used to be all about the data, users and decision makers have realized that big data cannot deliver much value on its own. Now, the focus is on how to unlock value in the big data—it is all about the *analytics*.

Big data without analysis yields no actionable information and intelligence that can be used to make decisions. Analytics seeks to discover patterns in data for decision making. It involves employing tools and techniques for uncovering useful insights into and extracting meaning from high-volume data streams and large data sets, and producing as results valuable data products for decision making. Analytical software and service products for analyzing data abound. The results are typically presented in the form of derivative data sets and interactive graphical user interface displays, such as dashboards.

Numerous analytics have been applied to problems in business and in the physical and social sciences. Up until 30 years ago, simple business models often sufficed for international business operational decision making. The advent of globalization, brought on partly due to advances in digital technology and massive amounts of information available at our fingertips, coupled with a rapidly changing, even chaotic, international political environment, have upended these models. Globalization has increased the diversity and uncertainty in outcomes when complex systems such as financial flows and markets, regional economies and political systems, and transnational threats involving multiple actors are in constant flux. These latter problems are often not quantitative, but qualitative, as the data to be processed is symbolic, textual, oral, visual, and animated/video-based.

Big Data Usage

Four years ago, we looked at the state of big data usage through the lens of multiple organizations that perform surveys of organizations and their executives. Since then, the big data landscape has changed dramatically. Everyone was speaking about big data, but now almost everyone is investing resources in applying big data techniques to support business operations and inform decision making.

Gigaspaces (2018) found that 80 percent of the business professionals it surveyed at industry trade shows reported that big data was important to their business operations, with 43 percent indicating that it was mission-critical. Bean (2017) surveyed executives of Fortune 1000 companies about their use of big data. He found that 48.4 percent of them were achieving measurable results from their big data investments. 80.7 percent of these executives characterized these investments as "successful." But, after the "quick wins," usually focused on cost reductions, achieving business-changing results takes more time, effort, and insights about how to apply big data techniques.

In a previous survey, Barth and Bean (2012) found a significant gap in capabilities, as the organizations perceived that they currently have limited abilities to address these expectations. Specifically, only 15 percent of respondents ranked their access to data today as adequate or world-class and only 21 percent of respondents ranked their analytic capabilities as adequate or world-class. Finally, only 17 percent of respondents ranked their ability to use data and analytics to transform their business as more than adequate or world-class.

It is important to note that the word "analytics" is often misinterpreted. Analytics expertise is often confused with the ability to use tools like Tableau, Excel, or other business intelligence (BI) tools. Others think of analytics as simply doing quantitative analysis. But these are just parts of the whole. Analytics has a full life cycle, which begins by formulating an analytics question or problem that can be answered or resolved with data.

These analytics questions are generally not easy to answer and require some knowledge of the domain in which the analysis is taking place. For example, to answer a marketing question, the analyst needs to have some knowledge and experience of marketing. That is, analytics does not happen in a vacuum. The analyst then needs to embark in a data quest to identify and gather all the necessary data to answer the question and then select the most appropriate modeling approach or combination of models most suitable to the task. Analysis and reporting of results comes at the very end of the cycle.

Figuring out an analytic approach to answer a question is not easy and this is where the analytics professional shines. Once an approach to answering the question has been identified, the analysis can then be automated with tools and this is the realm of "business intelligence."

As discussed earlier in this book, big data has the potential to provide significant benefits to an organization, including, but not limited to:

- Creating visibility into operations and processes
- Enabling experimentation to discover needs
- Improving organizational performance
- Helping gain deeper insight into organizational processes due to greater granularity
- Helping segment populations for targeted marketing actions
- Creating new business models, innovative processes and products, and services

Big data can improve decision making because: (1) there is more data to analyze, and (2) better data management and analysis environments are becoming available all the time. The difference between the information that managers view as important and necessary for decision making and the information that their organizations can provide to them can have a significant impact on decision making. The gap between information about customer needs and preferences is estimated to average 80 percent (Pricewaterhouse Coopers 2009).

New Vantage Partners (2018) has found that the resurgence in artificial intelligence (AI) associated with big data is a continuum, rather than separate technologies. To that end, 97 percent of their survey respondents indicated they are investing in big data and AI projects, and 73 percent said they had already received some measurable value from their investments. Most of these investments are focused on analytics to yield better decision making. 53.6 percent said they are investing in innovation projects, but these still remain an aspiration for most organizations. Monetization of these investments is a low priority with a low success rate.

Big Data Analytics

Organizations will find there is little value in just storing large amounts of data. True business value is created only when the data is captured, analyzed, and understood—relationships, trends, and patterns discovered that result in insights that produce better decision making and problem solving. Big data analytic applications need to be proactive, predictive, and have forecasting capabilities.

Currently the use of analytics as a competitive differentiator in selected industries is exploding. Disciplines such as marketing, sales, human resources, IT management, and finance are continuing to be transformed by the use of big data and analytics.

Before we start, we need to address some of the confusions that persist, especially with respect to terminology about different big data–related disciplines associated with analytics. Moreover, analytics can have a different scope or meaning depending on an individual's background. For example, is traditional data mining or BI a form of analytics? What is data science? And how is it different from analytics?

Let us start with the standard definition of *business Intelligence*: "Business Intelligence refers to the technologies, applications, and processes for gathering, storing, accessing, and analyzing data to help its users make better decisions" (Wixom and Watson 2010).

Next is *data mining*, which has traditionally been thought of as the computational process of discovering trends in data. It incorporates machine learning, statistics, and database systems. It is about extracting patterns and knowledge and identifying previously unknown relationships in the data (e.g., using cluster analysis for anomaly detections). It is good for hypotheses development. Some view data mining as the data exploration work done to identify interesting hypotheses, and analytics as the evaluation of those hypotheses.

You will also hear the term "data science" when big data is discussed. *Data science* "is a set of fundamental principles that guide the extraction of knowledge from data" (Provost and Fawcett 2013). A "data scientist" generally has deep knowledge of data mining analytics, a comprehensive view of the data, the discipline in which analysis is conducted (marketing, health care, social media, etc.), and the underlying core disciplines (e.g., statistics, mathematics, databases, etc.).

Industry leaders in online education have argued that there is no consensus about what these terms mean, at least in the educational market. As a McKinsey Global Institute study noted (Manyika et al. 2011), the US would face a talent shortage of 140,000 to 190,000 professionals with deep analytical skills, and about 1.5 million managers and decision makers with analytics skills. A follow-up study in 2016 by Gartner found that these shortage predictions were met and that average wages for data scientists grew by about 16 percent annually from 2012 to 2014. They projected a further shortage of 2 to 4 million "business translators", i.e., business professionals with analytics skills who can interact with data scientists (McKinsey Global Institute 2016). But the Bureau of Labor Statistics anticipated only 500,000 analytics-savvy managers from 2016 to 2024. The online education market views these deep analytical professionals as "data scientists" who have a well-rounded education in data-related disciplines and often hold PhD degrees in mathematics, statistics, management sciences, or other quantitative fields.

"Analytics" professionals are viewed as these business translators who also have deep quantitative backgrounds, but are perhaps one step below data scientists in terms of mathematical and data sophistication. "Business analytics professionals" appears to be the term of choice for the professionals required to make up the massive shortages described previously. These are either managers with deep expertise in the business domain of analysis (e.g., marketing, cyber security, public policy, etc.) who are trained in core analytics methods, or savvy consumers of analytics reports produced by data scientists, but who can complement these reports with further analysis of their own.

Rather than trying to parse these different definitions, we adopt a definition of big data analytics as focusing on helping managers gain improved insights about their business operations and make better, fact-based decisions.

The *Institute for Operations Research and Management Sciences* (INFORMS), the leading professional and academic organization in the analytics community, defines big data analytics as "the scientific process of transforming data into insight for making better decisions" (see https://www.informs.org/About-INFORMS/What-is-Analytics). We will stick with that definition in this booklet.

Big data analytics can be further be broken down as the use of:

- Large amounts of both structured and unstructured data, either at rest or in a streaming state
- Advanced information technology to support the analysis and modeling of data
- Statistical methods to provide rigor to the analysis
- Visual analysis to help discover patterns and trends in the data and present the results to key decision makers
- Other quantitative and qualitative methods, and mathematical or computer-based models

Following the infamous three Vs of big data, big data analytics (BDA) can also be viewed as doing analytics with large "volumes" of data, available in a "variety" of types and formats, as described in Table 1.1.

Another way to distinguish BDA from plain analytics is the environment in which the analysis is conducted. Figure 3.1 illustrates the differences between traditional analytics, analytics with big data, and BDA. One can do standard analytics work with big data by downloading the necessary data from large data warehouses and applying conventional analytics methods and tools. But this is not necessarily viewed as BDA. BDA is the practice of conducting analytics directly in the big data environments. This often requires programming skills, such as Java, Python, or R, and technologies like "in-memory" analytics, which are rapidly becoming mainstream. However, in some cases, when working with big data, analytics is not conducted directly on the big data per se. Instead,

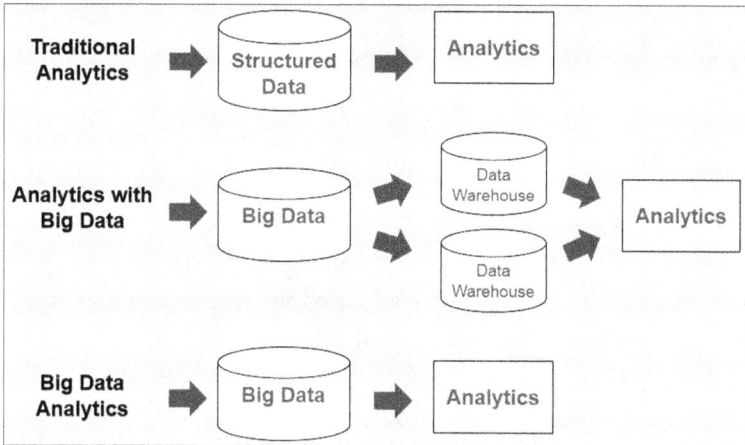

Figure 3.1 Big data analytics

the necessary data is extracted from traditional and nontraditional sources into a structured data warehouse or database for further manipulation and analysis.

Examples of big data analytics that can be applied in business organizations include:

- Management of customer relationships (free Wi-Fi)
- Financial and marketing activities (credit card drop)
- Supply chain management (find bottlenecks)
- Human resource planning (Hewlett Packard's flight risk score of its more than 300,000 employees)
- Pricing decisions (best price for a new product—Starbucks based these on analysis of tweets)
- Sports team game strategies (Moneyball)

However, big data is about more than just business analytics. For example, big data can transform:

- Medicine, including, but not limited to, processing 3-D hyperspectral high-resolution images for diagnostics, genomic research, proteomics, and so on

- Demographic analysis
- Geointelligence or spatial analysis

The term *advanced analytics* is utilized frequently in analytic circles. Advanced analytics uses both quantitative and qualitative methods such as data mining, predictive analytics, and simulation and optimization techniques, to produce insights and information that traditional approaches cannot. Our view is that advanced analytics goes beyond merely statistical mechanisms to a variety of other analytical methods which, combined in various ways, can offer considerable analytical power and insight into large sets of data. Appendix A lists our taxonomy of analytics classes (Kaisler et al. 2014). A few of the examples of the application of advanced analytics to big data are included in Table 3.1.

Table 3.1 Examples of advanced analytics

Big data production	Big data exploration	Traditional data production	Traditional data exploration
Predictive maintenance	Text analytics	Credit risk	Customer buying patterns
Real-time fraud detection	Image recognition	Telecom customer churn	Determine drivers of part failure
Predictive policing	Internet of Things	Product recommendations	Exploring anomalies, for example, new types of fraud
		Marketing response propensity	Customer segmentation

Big Data Analytics Initiatives Need a Process

When approaching a BDA initiative, successful outcomes are more likely if a process or analytics life cycle is followed. While activities will vary based on the type of problem you are trying to solve, the nature of the solution, and the nature of the data, they can be conducted in both agile and/or traditional environments. Key activities include those that follow and are also presented in Figure 3.2.

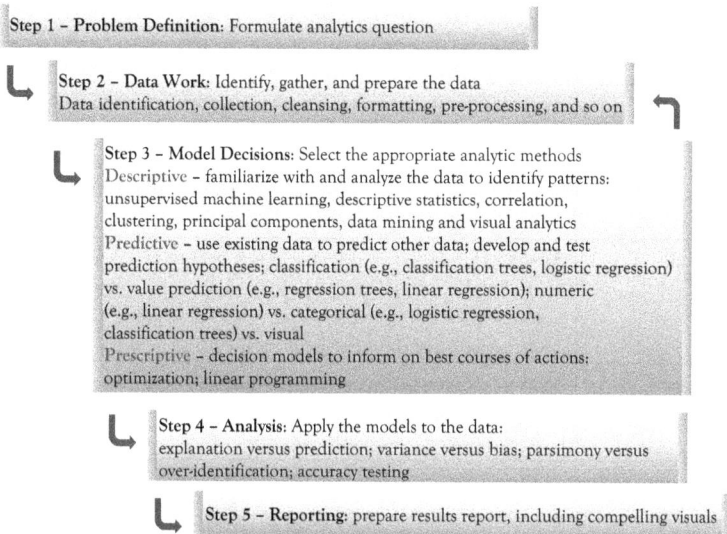

Figure 3.2 Key analytic life cycle activities

The Analytics Cycle

The *analytics life cycle* has many steps, which may vary depending on the problem at hand, but it typically involves five distinct steps or phases, depicted in Figure 3.1: (1) problem definition, (2) data work, (3) modeling decisions, (4) analysis, and (5) reporting. What is very telling about these five steps is that the actual analysis is only a small part of the full analytics cycle, and a lot of time needs to be devoted to analyzing the problem, preparing the data, and strategizing about the analytical approach to be used. We now discuss each of these steps in more detail.

Step 1—Problem Definition

What problem are you trying to solve? First, you need to formulate a business or domain question or problem that you wish to address. This will provide the needed direction to the effort of selecting data and performing analytics. What level of problem are you focusing on: operational, tactical, or strategic? Managers have different perspectives on analytics that depend on their business operations responsibilities and their level of decision making within an organization. Table 3.2 presents a brief description of these "levels" of analytic initiatives, which focus on the type of decision making within an organization.

Table 3.2 Business-focused analytics levels

Class	Description
Operational	Analytics that support day-to-day business operations, including monitoring and event data analytics leading to "here and now" metrics and near-term decision making. For example, dynamic product pricing based on customer purchasing patterns (Clifford 2012).
Tactical	Analytics focused on mid-term decision making and dealing with tactical problems, including simple predictive models based on historical data. For example, target's use of purchasing patterns to predict pregnancy in a teenage girl (Hill 2012).
Strategic	Analytics for long-term decisions, focused on organizational stability and directional decision making, including predictive, prescriptive, and comparative analytics.

One important aspect of the problem definition has to do with functional domain knowledge. Before we can frame and articulate an analytics question, the analyst needs to understand the functional domain of analysis. For example, it would be very difficult to build a predictive model for stock prices without having some fundamental knowledge of finance and the stock market. Similarly, in order to use analytics to detect and prevent cyber security breaches, the analyst needs to understand the cyber security domain.

The analytics question to be answered needs to have a well-defined objective but should also be somewhat general at this stage. For example, how can the company increase its market share by 1 percent? Which price will maximize profits for a particular type of new coffee beverage? As explained later in this chapter, the analyst will have to perform some descriptive analytics and be in a better position to translate the general analytics question into a number of more specific and testable analytics hypotheses.

Step 2—Data Work

This step involves the identification, gathering, cleansing, and preparation of the necessary data available to answer the question or problem. This can be the most time-consuming step in the entire analytics process. Analysts often spend 70 to 80 percent of their effort in this activity. As we have mentioned in earlier chapters, data can take many forms:

- Structured data "legacy"
- Unstructured data
- The "deep" web
- Data that is hidden in the enterprise
- Sensory data
- Analog devices turned digital

All data and analytics projects should begin with the question: What do you want to accomplish with your data? To organize and manage data, we must understand our data. When considering big data, we often only consider scale; for example, how much data we have. This affects our ability to acquire, store, and preserve data for future analysis. However, the complexity of data is often a large challenge as well; factors such as the complexity of the structure and semantics and the richness of data, and the complex relationships among data elements and structures will affect our ability to efficiently store and analyze data. Context and data reliability is normally required to understand the data and to establish accuracy, future usability, and so on.

A key question to answer is: What will yield more accurate results—sophisticated and complex models with poor-quality data or simple models with high-quality data? Naturally, this is a balancing act. But, the point most experts agree on is that nothing beats high-quality data. Bad data will only lead to poor predictions and no model's sophistication will be able to correct for bad data. Complex models are very difficult to understand, tune, and update, and often suffer from overfitting, dimensionality issues (e.g., multicollinearity) and high variance (i.e., resampling various training data subsets yield different results). Simpler, parsimonious models have the added advantage that they can provide more intuitive explanations of the relationships and patterns in the data, which are easier to explain and justify to a management audience. However, simpler models often suffer from high bias from omitted variables. Regardless, analysts need to spend a high proportion of the analytic life cycle time working with the data.

Whether data is maintained internally or gathered externally, there are two important processes that will follow: data cleansing and data preprocessing. Data cleansing has to do with making corrections for things like incorrect data, inconsistent data, redundancies, outliers, and missing data, among many other things.

Preprocessing has to do with the fact that raw data is rarely in the form needed for analytics. For example, often the necessary data is in multiple tables, in which case the analyst may have to join multiple data tables or link data elements as needed. Another type of preprocessing has to do with unstructured, text, and categorical data. Unstructured and text data are often preprocessed to construct structural variables for analysis. For example, if you are building a model to predict which e-mail messages are spam, the use of excessive capitalization is considered to be a good predictor. If you agree, then you could pre-process e-mail text to count the number of capitalized letters in the message.

With categorical data, the problem is that this type of data is not quantitative and therefore cannot be used as is with most statistical methods. But categorical data can often be converted into numerical data (e.g., male = 0, female = 1; urban = 0, suburban = 1, rural = 2). However, conversion may cause a loss of precision, fidelity, and accuracy of the data. Preprocessing is often needed too when the evaluation of the model shows problems with the data. For example, if the predictor variable data is skewed, you may not be able to use most traditional models like ordinary least squares regression, which requires that the predictor variable be normally distributed. However, skewed data can often be corrected by taking the log of the data, or rescaling the data. Other preprocessing transformations often used include: squared terms (x^2), inversed variable ($1/x$), interaction terms ($x_1 * x_2$), rank transformations (i.e., use the rank of the data rather than the data itself, which provides a more uniform distribution), and logistic functions (to predict categorical outcomes), among others.

Step 3—Modeling Decisions

In this step, modeling is performed to understand and explore the data as well as to then predict and prescribe outcomes based on the data. There are multiple approaches on modeling decisions, including the following:

- *Analysis types*: descriptive, predictive, or prescriptive
- *Modeling type*: numerical associations or categorical
- *Analysis approach*: structured, unstructured, visual, or mixed
- *Statistical learning type*: unsupervised or supervised learning

Analysis Types

When modeling a decision via analytics, one typically has to answer several basic questions:

- What has happened?
- What is likely to happen?
- What can we do when it happens?
- Why did it happen?

To answer these questions, one uses several categories of analytical types of approaches, and these include descriptive, predictive, and prescriptive analytics to quantitatively and qualitatively model the data. Descriptive or visual models are used to cognitively improve the results of the models. These modeling approaches are to be used as appropriate for the specific business problem that is being solved. These types are discussed in Table 3.3.

Table 3.3 Analytic modeling categories

Type	Description
Descriptive	Descriptive: getting meaning from the data—for example, BlueFin Technologies: Did viewers like a particular TV show last night, based on tweets? Are variables normally distributed or skewed? Are predictors correlated? A set of techniques for reviewing and examining the data set(s) to explore and understand the data determine what has happened and find the patterns: How many, when, where? Often uses data mining and clustering techniques.
Predictive	Predictive: using some variables in the data to predict the outcome of others—for example, Target: Which product purchases are the best predictors of the likelihood that a female customer is expecting a baby? A set of techniques that analyze current and historical data to determine what is most likely to happen or not: What could happen next if . . .? What actions are needed? Often uses regression methods, time series models, and statistical machine-learning techniques.
Prescriptive	Prescriptive: using the data to recommend what to do to achieve outcomes—for example, Starbucks: What is the optimal price of a new coffee brand to maximize sales? A set of techniques for developing and analyzing alternatives computationally, which can become courses of action—either tactical or strategic: What are the possible outcomes? How can we achieve the best outcome? What if we do . . .? Often uses operations research methods, decision modeling, symbolic machine learning, simulation, and system dynamics.

Descriptive Analytics.   Descriptive analytics allows you to consolidate big data into smaller, more useful subsets of information. Big data is not suitable for human understanding, but the information we derive from the data is.

Descriptive analytics' real power is that it allows you to familiarize yourself with the data (utilize descriptive statistics, correlations, factor analysis, cluster analysis, etc. to better understand the data), as well as start to generate possible hypotheses (via data mining, patterns, trends, etc.). Any analytic method aimed at understanding the data or evaluating possible associations, classifications, or relationships falls in the category of descriptive analytics.

While data mining is not used exclusively for descriptive analytics, it is often used to uncover previously unidentified relationships in the data. There are many descriptive analytics methods and describing all of them is way beyond the scope of this booklet, but some examples include: descriptive statistics—which provide various statistical parameters for the data (e.g., mean, minimum, maximum, standard deviation)—frequency distributions, correlation among variables, analysis, factor analysis (through principal components), cluster analysis, and classification trees.

Predictive Analytics.   Predictive analytics is by far the most popular type because the very reason why we embark on an analytics project is usually to be able to anticipate outcomes. Basically, you take data that you have, to predict data you do not have. However, descriptive analytics should often precede predictive analytics because it is important that the analysts get immersed in the data to develop familiarity with it and identify trends and associations that were previously unknown. Descriptive analytics should help the analyst translate the general analytics question(s) for the problem at hand into more specific testable hypotheses that can be evaluated with predictive models.

One analytics question may result in several testable hypotheses. For example, an analytics question like "what are the best predictors of stock price?" may lead to various analytic hypotheses, such as: a stock's price-earnings ratio today will have a positive effect on the stock's price one year from now; the company size is a predictor of stock price stability;

the number of years in business is a predictor of stock price stability; technology stocks are generally overpriced; and so on. Each one of these hypotheses can be tested with a specific predictive model.

Most literature on predictive analytics emphasizes predictive accuracy. However, predictive accuracy needs to be well understood. For example, certain methods like classification trees can achieve 100 percent predictive accuracy through overidentification. The reason for this is that accuracy is often tested with the existing data. Machine-learning methods help overcome these problems through cross-validation, which involves partitioning data sets into training set (i.e., the portion of the data used to build the model) and testing set (i.e., the remaining data used to test the accuracy of the model) subsamples. There are many different methods to partition the data into training and testing sets, and evaluate the model accuracy. For example, you could partition the data randomly using an arbitrary threshold (e.g., 80 percent training set, 20 percent testing set). Another method could be to construct multiple training/testing sets to evaluate the predictive accuracy with multiple partitions. Yet another one could just "leave one observation out" and train the model with the rest of the data, and then test the model with the one observation left out, and then repeat this process multiple times. And yet another approach is to conduct Monte Carlo experiments to analyze the dispersion of data values and their effect upon results.

Complex and sophisticated models can be developed such that the predictive model touches every data point in the sample and, therefore, any accuracy testing will yield 100 percent accuracy. These models are said to be *overidentified*. But this makes the model exceedingly complicated, making it very difficult to use it to explain relationships in the data. But more importantly, internal accuracy is no guarantee that the model will provide accurate predictions with new data. Testing models with new data is not about predictive accuracy, but about testing the external validity of the model.

Consequently, a sound predictive model needs to balance three things: (1) parsimony, that is, model simplicity that can provide useful intuitive explanations (e.g., a 10 percent decrease in a stock's price-earnings ratio leads to a 3 percent stock price increase a year later), (2) predictive accuracy, and (3) external validity.

At this point the analyst needs to formulate the necessary predictive hypotheses and the appropriate predictive analytic models and methods. These can include multivariate regression, logistic regression, forecasting, nonlinear models, classification trees, neural networks, and so on. Predictive models generally fall under two categories: predictions of values (e.g., future sales) and predictions about classification (e.g., will a loan client default on the loan or not?). We discuss this further in the next section.

However, as Michael Wu of Lithium Technologies (www.lithium .com) has pointed out:

> The purpose of predictive analytics is NOT to tell you what will happen in the future. It cannot do that. In fact, no analytics can do that. Predictive analytics can only forecast what might happen in the future, because all predictive analytics are probabilistic in nature.

Well, not all, but most of the ones currently popular in the public blogosphere and online technical articles are statistical in nature.

Advances in machine learning have really improved our ability to make accurate predictions in a number of ways: (1) ability to model the problem with multiple models using various approaches and test them rigorously through cross-validation (i.e., fit each model with various training subsamples and test their predictive deviance, and select the most accurate model); (2) increased model sophistication (e.g., regression and classification trees are notoriously inaccurate predictive models, but newer versions, using various forms of random resampling like Bootstrap Aggregation, Random Forest, and Boosted Trees, allow the analyst to quickly run hundreds or thousands of train-test cycles to improve predictive accuracy dramatically); (3) ability to assemble models in which the analyst is not confined to a single model, but can make more accurate predictions by averaging the prediction of several models; (4) ability to automate any of the three approaches above to be able to refit models as the data changes (e.g., Amazon learning from your purchase habits to predict what you are likely to buy and then use this data to make recommendations).

Prescriptive Analytics.   Prescriptive analytics uses optimization and simulation algorithms to advise on possible outcomes and answers: "What should we do?" Prescriptive analytics may also be used to assess different courses of action and their likely outcomes.

Prescriptive analytics uses a combination of modeling approaches such as business rules, machine learning, and computational modeling procedures, among others, which can be run against historical and trans-actional data, and real-time data feeds. You then identify and develop decision and optimization models incorporating domain knowledge to develop possible outcomes and rank them in some way so that the best possible outcome, given the inputs, emerges from the mix of outcomes. The prescriptive model can also suggest or recommend one or more pos-sible courses of action, ranking them according to some set of constraints.

But one must remember what some called the MD^3 rule: *Models Don't Make Decisions, Managers Do!!!* That is, unless the prescriptive models are implemented in an automated application (e.g., to recommend products to buy based on prior purchase history), prescriptive models should be viewed as aids to human decision making. Humans should make their own decisions, aided by prescriptive models, but the prescribed decisions should not be followed blindly.

Modeling Types

There are several modeling types, but they can be succinctly classified as either numerical or categorical. *Numerical models* are generally based on correlation and associations of the various variables relevant for the analysis. Numerical models for descriptive analytics include things such as descriptive statistics, clustering analysis, factor analysis through prin-cipal components, correlation analysis, and analysis of frequencies and distributions, among others. Numerical models for prescriptive analytics include things such as multiple regression analysis, regression trees, struc-tural equation models, and neural networks, among others.

Categorical models are generally based on classifications in the data. For example, students in a university data file may be classified as freshmen, sophomores, juniors, seniors, and graduates. Such categorizations do not lend themselves to quantitative analysis. But these categories are often transformed into numerical values or comparison groups where quantita-tive methods can be applied.

Categorical models for descriptive analytics include things such as analysis of variance (ANOVA) in which the means and variances of two or more categories are compared, and chi-square tests in which category counts can be analyzed and compared, among others. Categorical models for predictive analytics are referred to as "classification" models, and they include things such as logistic regression models, in which the predicted variable is categorical (e.g., default on loan vs. no default) but is converted into a quantitative value for analysis (e.g., no default = 0; default = 1); classification trees, in which the data is partitioned using predictor variables and the categories that fall in each partition are analyzed and further subpartitioned.

Analysis Approach

The analysis approach is based on the nature of the data being analyzed and it can be structured, unstructured, visual, or mixed. Structured data is data that can be easily organized in tables with columns, such that each column contains data of the same type (e.g., numerical value with two decimal points; text with up to 16 characters; dates in dd/mm/yyyy format). Structured data generally contains numerical data, which can be analyzed with statistical methods, and categorical data, which can be classified with numerical values.

Unstructured data refers to data that does not have many restrictions in what it can contain, except for the type of data. For example, text data is considered unstructured, but it is restricted to text only. Similarly, video data is also unstructured, but it can only contain video footage. There are essentially two ways to analyze unstructured data: using unstructured data analysis methods or developing some structured metadata from the unstructured data and then using structured data analysis methods.

More and more software tools and methods are being introduced to analyze unstructured data. For example, there is an abundance of text mining tools that can process millions of pages, uncovering patterns in the data by identifying themes. Because words can have various meanings, there is an abundance of synonym files customized to particular industries. Unstructured data can often be processed to give it some structure for analysis. For example, a data set with movies will generally have some metadata associated with it, with information like actors, producer, director, release year, duration, minutes on screen for each actor, movie segments with timeline pointers, and so on. Similarly, text data can have things like word counts, frequency of usage for words, or a combination of words of interest.

A picture is worth a thousand words. *Visual analytics* is the science of analytical reasoning facilitated by interactive visual interfaces. It is also a set of techniques for visualizing information to facilitate human decision making. The field of visual analytics is maturing rapidly with very sophisticated tools like Tableau and SAP's Lumira coming to the market all the time. For example, IBM has an advanced visualization website (http://www-01.ibm.com/software/analytics/many-eyes/), which provides a number of very clever web-based visualization tools for free.

Statistical Learning.   Statistical learning is related to the concept of machine learning discussed above. Machine learning is often thought of as the science of getting computers to act without being explicitly programmed. Statistical learning is the application of statistical methods to support machine learning. For example, getting an e-mail system to identify spam is an application of statistical learning. In simpler terms, statistical learning refers to the ability of computer models to learn patterns from the data. Models are "trained" with the data, and as new data comes in, the models can learn the new patterns. In very simple terms, running a regression model and estimating coefficients that explain a predictor variable is a form of statistical learning. As new data is collected, the regression models can be reestimated to produce new coefficients. In essence, many numeric analytic models are created by applying machine-learning methods.

Developing coefficients that can explain relationships in the data is referred to as "learning." Such learning can be of two types: unsupervised and supervised. Unsupervised learning refers to machine-learning methods in which the outcome is not known or there is no specific goal for this outcome. For example, when an analyst looks at sales data and discovers surprisingly that beer and diapers sell well together, he or she is employing unsupervised learning methods. Examples of unsupervised learning methods include things like cluster analysis, classification algorithms, correlation analysis, and multidimensional scaling, and are most typically employed in descriptive analytics. In supervised learning, the outcome of interest is specified and there is a specific goal for the analysis outcomes. For example, when an analyst is trying to predict which advertising approaches lead to increased sales, he or she is employing supervised learning methods. Examples of supervised learning methods include things such as regression analysis, regression trees, classification trees, and neural networks and are most typically employed in predictive analytics.

Step 4—Analysis

We are often asked by nonanalytical professionals to describe what analytics is. Inevitably, when we answer this question using an INFORMS definition—that is, to extract meaning from the data for decision making—most people then ask, "What is new?" Or they make comments like, "But we have been doing this for years," and they are right. The work analysts do in the analysis step is no different from the work that statisticians, data miners, and decision modelers have been doing for years.

What distinguishes analytics from these other fields are two main things: (1) analytics is more than analysis and it includes all aspects of the life cycle described in this chapter; and (2) analytics incorporates a confluence of various fields that were previously viewed as different, including statistics, mathematical modeling, quantitative sciences, data mining, software programming (e.g., computational statistics), database and big data, management sciences, and decision sciences, among many others. But all activities in the life cycle have a single purpose, which is to support the analysis that will answer the analytics question at hand.

Analysis is often performed by humans executing statistical, data mining or statistical learning algorithms with increasingly more sophisticated tools. This analysis is semiautomated. For example, a predictive model designed to catch spam e-mail is running in the background by some mail server feature, without human intervention. During the training period, the analyst may have provided feedback to the algorithm about good or bad choices leading to results. Or, a company like Amazon may be running predictive models in the background to make customized purchase recommendations to customers. Humans intervene in these cases to tune the parameters of the models from time to time, but the analytics models are executed automatically by a software program.

One important aspect in analysis is the selection of the appropriate analytic tools. Tools can be proprietary and expensive, but there are an increasing number of free open source software (OSS) systems. It is becoming difficult to select the appropriate tools because of the overwhelming number of them in the market. We present some of the tools in common use today in Volume II.

Step 5—Reporting

This step involves writing up the results, conclusions, and recommendations for the audience interested in the respective analytics question. Conclusions and recommendations must be documented, and these findings presented at a level and in a format that end users will find understandable. It is important to note that analytics is a quantitative and highly technical discipline and, therefore, many high-level managers, clients, and stakeholders may not have the background to understand statistical output. A well-articulated report that contains the main findings, conclusions, and recommendations will go a long way.

Analytics reports are often accompanied by attractive visuals and graphics. But we often get confused or overwhelmed when the report contains an overwhelming amount of graphics without proper explanations. To maximize the impact and the business value of the analytics report, we recommend a few important guidelines in Table 3.4.

Table 3.4 Selected guidelines for analytic reporting

Reports should have a text narrative that briefly describes the analytics question, hypotheses, data sources, and methods employed.
The report should contain a well-written and well-articulated explanation of key findings, and state whether the hypotheses were supported or not.
Supported hypotheses should have a brief commentary, and unsupported hypotheses should have an intuitive rationale or explanation for why the expected results were not found, or why they had effects opposite to the predicted direction.
No graphic or visual exhibit should be unexplained, and they should all be referenced and introduced in the main text—isolated visual exhibits that do not contribute or complement the narrative are generally useless and even distracting.
All visual exhibits should have all the necessary information in the exhibit to understand it—the most common omission in our experience is an explanation of the vertical or horizontal axes in the graph.

Analytic Modeling Methods and Approaches

There are a wide variety of analytical modeling methods and approaches available to the analyst when analyzing big data. It is not possible to identify and describe all of them, so we will highlight the most commonly used methods below.

Quantitative Analysis

Qualitative analytics approaches are primarily statistical or mathematically based. These techniques include linear regression analysis to analyze continuous dependent variables; logistic regression to analyze binary or categorical dependent variables, classification trees, such as decision trees; correlation; data reduction; and so on. Other techniques include:

- Associations: correlation among variables, ANOVA, regression models, which variables covary with which—for example, how much does annual income increase with each year of additional university education?
- Classification (and probability estimation): in which class does a case belong (predicting the probability that a new case will fall in a given class); chi-square analysis, logistic regression models—for example, patient tested positive (or negative) for a disease; what are the probabilities of testing positive for a disease?
- Others: clustering, similarity matching, co-occurrence grouping, profiling, link (strength) prediction, data reduction (factor analysis), causal modeling, and so on.

Qualitative Analysis

Qualitative analysis commonly refers to relatively unstructured, nondirective discussions or interviews (such as focus groups, depth interviews, and ethnography or observation) to explore a topic. It can use subjective judgment based on nonquantifiable information.

Visual Analytics

Visual analytics is driving new ways of presenting data and information to the user. Wong and Thomas (2004) defined it as follow: "Visual analytics is the formation of abstract visual metaphors in combination with a human information discourse (interaction) that enables detection of the expected and discovery of the unexpected within massive, dynamically changing information spaces." In 2005, a scientific panel defined it as "the science of analytical reasoning facilitated by interactive visual interfaces" (Thomas and Cook 2005).

It is important to note that while we are describing visual analytics as a specific analytic approach, it actually permeates all types of analyses. For example, descriptive, predictive, and prescriptive analytics' results are often accompanied by powerful graphics that convey results very clearly. A picture is worth a thousand words. Visual analytics is often viewed as providing visual renditions of the available data and analytic model results (e.g., pie charts, scatterplots, and social network diagrams). But the true power of visual analytics is in actually employing visual methods to present easy interpretations of predictions and prescriptions, not just descriptions of data, due to the sophistication of the eye–brain interaction. As humans, we can quickly grasp information presented graphically as opposed to information presented via text or columns of numbers.

Visualization is a very old and mature science. All analytical tools have features to prepare charts, box plots, distribution curves, pie charts, and line graphs with trends. So this is not new. What is new is the level of sophistication that is constantly being added to existing tools and new ones arriving in the market all the time. For example, statistical analysis software (SAS) has a full suite of visual analytics tools. Other tools like Tableau specialize specifically in visualization, but like many other visual analytics tools, it offers the capability of running statistics and other quantitative methods from within the tool. For example, Tableau allows users to load and run R scripts to estimate statistical models like multiple regressions, which can then be visualized in many ways by the tool.

Visualization has long been used for data representation. Nothing illustrates a point better than a well-prepared slide show full of interesting graphics. As visualization expert Tufte noted: "graphical excellence is that which gives to the viewer the greatest number of ideas in the shortest time with the least ink in the smallest space" (Tufte 2001, The Visual Display of Quantitative Information). But visual analytics has taken this to the next step by also providing ways to conduct the actual analysis visually. For example, visual analysis has a long tradition in social network analysis.

Tools like Krackplot, NetDraw (free), and Pagent have been around for several years to illustrate how actors in a social network interconnect. For example, identifying the most central actor in a network can often be done much easier visually than statistically. Similarly, modern visualization tools like Tableau, Lumira, and ggplot2 for R are helping analysts develop compelling visual models with little effort.

Similarly, popular sites providing interesting and intuitive visual analysis websites are rapidly appearing, including https://infogram/, http://www-01.ibm.com/software/analytics/many-eyes, and www.informationis beautiful.net. There are also many scientific and prominent conferences devoted to visualization, not just visual analytics, including http://ieeevis .org/ and http://s2015.siggraph.org/.

Emerging Analytics Application Areas

New application analytics are being developed continually and are moving beyond the simple statistical approaches in data mining. New infrastructure has provided an ability to process information from sources that were previously the focus of research. New analytics are based on advanced mathematical, engineering, and computer science techniques that incorporate models and data from social, demographic, political, and other scientific disciplines.

Social analytics often focus on intangible and qualitative phenomena with varying parameters and interdisciplinary contexts. Sometimes, the data is not directly measurable but must be determined through proxy variables that can be imprecise and uncertain. The data may be nonnumeric, thus requiring reduction and encoding to numeric values, but may lose precision and information as a result.

Social network analytics (SNA) focuses on analyzing actors or other network nodes and the relationships or ties among them. It is widely used in areas like social media analysis, cyber security (link) analysis, epidemics, and political analysis. SNA can offer interesting insights into relationship data at various levels, including: network node (e.g., actor prominence in the network, power, ability to broker relationships, bridging roles, ego networks, etc.); dyad relationship (e.g., reciprocity, weak vs. strong tie effects, bridging relationships, etc.); subgroup (e.g., effects of cliques, network components, clusters, communities, etc.); network structure (e.g., effects of network hierarchy, centralization, density, diameter, etc.); and multiplex network associations (e.g., effect of various network relationships, such as friendship and report-to, to other network relation outcomes, such as advice-seeking behavior).

Behavioral analytics focuses on understanding and predicting human behavior in various areas of human interaction, such as behavior, personnel management, and online gaming behavior, among others. The goal in behavior analytics is to develop accurate models to predict how humans act or are likely to act and why.

Cognitive analytics is the application of human-like knowledge and intelligence to make predictions that mimic the decisions of experts using machine-learning algorithms.

Global business problems are a mix of physical and social problems, but are strongly influenced by social phenomena. Hence, a mix of physical and social analytics must be developed and applied to model and understand business operations in the global environment. Kaisler and Cioffi-Revilla (2007) reviewed a set of analytical methods and classified them into 17 classes. Kaisler (2012) extended that analysis to the problem of intelligence analysis. Appendix A briefly describes these classes.

Sentiment Analysis

Sentiment analysis mines data streams to determine trending issues. It attempts to determine demographic, social, and customer sentiments regarding issues and how they relate to products. A hefty dose of psychology accompanied by behavioral models is the current approach.

There is a goldmine of information being collected by service organizations—both customer-focused and across the web. One use of this data is to gauge the collective consciousness of the respective populations. On the one hand, an organization can assemble and assess a variety of sentiments based on customer orders, complaints, comments, and even blogs devoted to specific products or organizations. Online opinion has become a powerful force that can make or break a product in the marketplace or an organization's reputation through information or disinformation. On the other hand, an organization can assess different types of trends based on a broad collection across the web.

Sentiment analysis is an emerging field that attempts to analyze and measure human emotions and convert them into symbolic and quantitative data. In either case above, organizations monitor news articles, online forums (blogs, chat rooms, twitter feeds, etc.), and social networking sites for trends in opinions about their products and services, or for topics in the news that may affect their business decisions or operations. Sentiment analysis is one example of the field of social analytics.

Generally, sentiment analysis uses raw text as its input. Sentiment analysis works by classifying the polarity of a given text—whether tweet, blog entry, or document—either in part or in full. The simplest algorithms work by scanning keywords in the text to categorize a statement as negative, neutral, or positive, based on a simple binary analysis. For example, "enjoyed" is good, but "miserable" is bad. The individual scores for words, phrases, sentences, and documents—whatever units you use—are then combined to form an overall sentiment for the set of data that you have. You can interpret the final score based on the domain you are working in. For example, if you sampled sportswriters' tweets regarding athletes at the London Olympics as one of us did, you can get a "sentiment" of who the preferred athletes were in several of the major sports.

However, not all opinions are equally important. Some pundits carry more weight because of their stature in the business community, the number of times they have ordered products or services from the company, or their popularity, for example, as measured by the number of followers. A tweet by a famous actress or popular music artist will have much more impact than that by a person who has used a product or service just a few times. Thus, organizations must also develop profiles of commenters and rank their importance to generate weights when assessing comments.

As an example, a restaurant gathers tweets about its menu and service. It identifies tweeters who have large numbers of followers and, perhaps, the number of times that have actually visited the restaurant and the number of different selections made. Tweeters with greater numbers in each case would be given greater importance in assessing their sentiments. Also, the number of retweets would measure the level of engagement with their followers and the degree of their influence. Using this technique the restaurant could identify opinion shapers of importance to them, assign them higher weights to calculate a more accurate indicator of sentiment, and engage them to correct negative impressions and to generate more positive impressions.

There are many challenges in applying sentiment analysis to a selection of text. Most tools use simple assignments to individual words. For example, the words "sinful" and "decadent" are often positive sentiments when applied to a chocolate confection obtained from a bakery, but have negative connotations in other instances. Most algorithms cannot handle irony, slang, jargon, or idioms—leading to erroneous polarity assignments that can skew the sentiment assigned to a text. Reliable sentiment analysis is going to require many linguistic shades of gray.

It should not replace opinion polling or other structured opinion assessment techniques, but it can complement their results due to the law of large numbers. In sentiment analysis, one does not have accurate control over the sample space, so the results are often hard to verify and validate. At best, they can show trends in real time whereas other techniques often take days to produce results.

Geospatial Analytics

Geospatial analytics (or *Location analytics*) expressly integrates geographic and demographic information into the analysis process. It applies statistical processing to data associated with geographical and demographical information, such as maps, census areas, mineral deposits, and so on. Many of the complex problems in BI, social science, and government have a geographic component that is often best expressed through visual analytics. There has been an explosion of applications at the intersection of mobile technology, GPS, machine learning, and geospatial analytics.

Geospatial analytics often incorporates a temporal dimension into the analysis process to complement the spatial dimension. For example, a retailer may want to analyze year-over-year sales per store to determine the best-performing stores. With these results, the retailer may take corrective actions at underperforming stores based on demographic analysis, perhaps even closing stores that do not have the ability to increase sales. Similarly, health care organizations can use spatial and temporal analysis to track and predict the spread of diseases. Such techniques were used to determine where to commit resources in the recent Ebola outbreak in Africa.

Unstructured Text Processing

With over 80 percent of the world's knowledge residing in unstructured text, whether on paper or in electronic form, the capability to process it to extract data and information is essential. Typical methods rely on statistical or symbolic natural language processing (NLP) and, sometimes, a hybrid of the two. Neither type is new as NLP research has been ongoing for over four decades, supported by the Defense Advanced Research Projects Agency (DARPA), National Science Foundation (NSF), and academia. Within the past decade or so, many commercial firms have discovered that developing tools for processing unstructured text is a viable market.

One of the major issues with NLP is ambiguity. For example, in English, many nouns and verbs have several close synonyms. The word *strike* has over 30 common meanings. In another example, there are more than 45,000 people in the United States named "John Smith." *Entity resolution* is the process of resolving a name to an explicit individual. In a series of articles, John Talburt (2009) identified a hierarchy of five methods for entity resolution ranging from simple deterministic matching to asserted or knowledge-based matching. As one ascends the hierarchy, the complexity of the processing required increases. Some of the symbolic classes are more flexible in using ambiguous data.

Resolving ambiguous data at higher levels requires domain knowledge to make decisions about the cause of ambiguity within the data. Assuming default values when encountering ambiguous data can lead to erroneous results. However, analysis and reasoning, as at the highest level of Talburt's hierarchy, may require intensive computation that affects performance. The tradeoff becomes end-to-end processing time for large quantities of data versus the fidelity and quality of individual data items.

Image, Video, and Audio Processing

With more data and information being recorded in images and video streams due to the ubiquity of cellphones and tablets with embedded cameras, a major percentage of the world's knowledge is becoming represented by image and video data. Granted a lot of it may be currently frivolous, but it is becoming a major influence given the success of services such as FaceBook, YouTube, SnapChat, InstaGram, Pinterest, Tumblr, and other social media.

Extracting information from imagery and full motion videos is very much a major research problem, but one that has significant potential for providing data for social and behavioral models that can lead to trends and customer preferences. Many organizations have been exploring and researching this for years, but this is still an extremely difficult problem to solve computationally, although the human mind, brain, and eye do it extremely well. While unstructured text remains the largest repository of big data, imagery and video are a strong second.

Another very difficult problem is finding ways to extract information from audio recordings such as telephone conversations and the audio tracks accompanying full motion video recordings. Most current audio processing systems do not process free-range speech, but rely on phrases chosen from distinct vocabularies.

Edge and Location-Specific Analytics

Because moving large amounts of data in the order of petabytes can be both time- and bandwidth-consuming, an emerging discipline is edge analytics, which also incorporates location-specific analytics. It may not be physically possible or economically feasible to store all the data streaming in at the endpoints of an organization's data and information network. Moreover, data perishability may be a significant factor if the lifetime of the data is less than the transport time from the endpoints to where it might be processed. One of the maxims of enterprise architecture is to place the processing (at least, the initial stages) close to where the data is collected, following, if possible, the 80–20 rule.

Edge analytics is focused on moving analytics to the frontier of the domain. For example, many cameras contain image processing functions that can be done right in the camera before you download the images. It is estimated that there is one camera for every 11 individuals in the United Kingdom. London is replete with cameras—some obvious and some not. With Google Glass beginning to shape the future of body-worn video cameras, significant issues in privacy, processing, and ownership of data are going to emerge that have yet to be addressed. Key questions include: What will we do with all this video? How will we process it? How will we store it (Satyanarayanan et al. 2015)?

Network Analytics

Social network analysis methods and tools have been around for many years. With the explosion of social media in the last several years, SNA has increased substantially in popularity. But social network analysis methods can be used for other types of network analysis that are not necessarily social.

Network analysis is derived from the field of "graph theory" and it has a rich tradition of quantitative and visual methods. A network can be represented mathematically as a table called a "sociomatrix" or an "adjacency matrix" by listing all members of the network in rows and in columns. The cells in the sociomatrix contain numerical values that measure some relation of interest between the row member and the column member (i.e., relation between "adjacent" members). The same network can be represented visually in "sociograms" by depicting each member as a node in a graph and then adding connecting lines representing the relationship between nodes (i.e., cells in the sociomatrix). These are called "one-mode" networks because rows and columns represent the same thing (e.g., friends on a social network).

However, networks can also be "two-mode" in which the rows contain the members and the columns contain some affiliation that members have. For example, if one were to list all the students in a university, one per row, and create a column for each course taught by the university, a two-mode network can be created by entering 1 in the respective cell indicating if the student took that course or 0 if he/she did not. The interesting thing about two-mode networks is that they can be de-composed (or "projected") into two one-mode networks, row-wise (e.g., student by student) or column-wise (e.g., course by course), which could help, for example, determine how students cluster together around fields of education, or how courses cluster together based on student enrollments. A similar analysis can be done with the infamous beer and diapers example showing that these two products are often purchased together at convenience stores. This can be analyzed by listing all transactions in rows and the products purchased in columns (a two-mode matrix). A column-wise one-mode projection would yield a product-by-product matrix that can be analyzed with methods like hierarchical clustering to evaluate which products are purchased together more often.

A full discussion of network analytics is beyond the scope of this book, but suffice it to say that there is a very rich and abundant set of quantitative and visual tools and methods to analyze dyadic relationships in networks.

Cognitive Analytics

Recently, a new type of analytics—*cognitive analytics*—exemplified by IBM's Watson, has emerged. Cognitive analytics exemplify the potential for machines to actually learn from experience inspired by how the human brain processes information, draws conclusions, and codifies instincts and experience into learning. It often uses concepts from deep machine learning, which focus on how the human brain learns and attempts to translate those techniques into software mechanisms.

IBM has created its System G Cognitive Analytics Toolkit (http:// systemg.research.ibm.com/cognitiveanalytics.html), which builds upon its decades of research in machine learning to provide a wide range of tools to detect humans' emotions and perceptions on text, images, or videos. IBM's visual sentiment and recognition tools can detect visual objects, such as faces, in images or videos and predict the feelings expressed. Their text emotion tool uses supervised learning to classify unstructured text into one of 12 categories.

IBM's Watson, a Jeopardy winner, is being converted to a general-purpose tool and applied to many different disciplines. A new product, Watson Analytics, "is like a data scientist in a box," according to Marc Altshuller, vice president of IBM Watson Analytics (http://searchdatamanagement.techtarget .com/news/2240238506/IBM-works-to-deliver-on-Watsons-cognitive-computing-promise). It is a subset of the analytics embedded in Watson that focuses on analytical discovery.

Key Challenges for Analytics

BDA is clearly here to stay. However, BDA is still in an emerging state in many respects. Perhaps the biggest challenge for success in big data is the lack of analytical professionals and managers who understand and can make decisions based on big data insights. This is changing rapidly due to the ensuing explosion of data science and analytics programs at universities, online education sites, and training institutions. Nevertheless, as a recent McKinsey Global (2016) report projected, there will be a demand of 2 to 4 million "business translators" over the next decade. These translators are either data scientists who understand business well, or business professionals with sound data science skills.

For example, industry, academia, and government currently suffer from a lack of analytical talent. Training, growing, and organizing big data professionals within an organization will be one of the key challenges to successful BDA initiatives going forward. We will discuss these and other organizational and people issues in Chapter 4.

Another key challenge in BDA includes the continued development and deployment of analytic tools that support business managers, analysts, and other "non" data scientist individuals to efficiently and successfully analyze outcomes. As mentioned earlier, the greatest amount of effort in a typical analytics initiative is in extracting, moving, cleaning, and preparing the data, not in actually analyzing it. As big data sources become larger, more complex, and more numerous, approaches to addressing this problem will become critical.

Table 3.5 presents other selected BDA challenges (Kaisler et al. 2013).

Table 3.5 Selected big data analytics challenges

Quantity vs. quality: What data is required to satisfy a given value proposition? At what precision and accuracy?
Tracking data and information provenance from data generation through data preparation and processing to derived data and information
Performing data validation and verification, including accuracy, precision, and reliability
Coping with sampling biases and heterogeneity
Using more diverse data, not just more data (Feinleb 2012)
Working with and integrating data having different formats and structures
Developing scalable algorithms to exploit current and emerging parallel and distributed architectures
Developing methods for visualizing massive data
Ensuring data sharing with security and integrity
Enabling data and information discovery
Understanding that approximate results given limited computational capacity are better than no results
Determining whether more data is better than better algorithms.

Finally, do not disregard traditional analytics; traditional and big data analytics will coexist for years to come.

Analytical Resource and Tool Survey

Analytical tools are packaged applications that allow users to begin working with data without having to do any programming. This will be a very brief survey of some of the different types of tools available. Managers need some familiarity with these tools, even if they do not fully understand how they work, in order to be able to discuss cogently with their IT support staff.

The available analytics resources and tools are expanding at an explosive rate. It is not possible, in a document this size, to list them all. The following section lists some of the resources and tools that the authors have used.

Commercial Packages

There are numerous commercial packages that now incorporate big data analytic capabilities—too many to list them all here. Although some of the authors have had experience with some of these packages, we are *not* endorsing any of them. Table 3.6 presents a few of these.

Table 3.6 Selected commercial packages

Package and website	Brief description
SAS http://www.sas.com/en_us/home.html	SAS is a software suite developed by SAS Institute for advanced analytics, BI, data management, and predictive analytics. See also: SAS Enterprise Guide http://support.sas.com/software/products/guide/index.html SAS Enterprise Miner http://www.sas.com/en_us/software/analytics/enterprise-miner.html
IBM SPSS http://www-01.ibm.com/software/analytics/spss	SPSS started out as a suite of statistical processing techniques, but has significantly expanded into the BDA domain. See also: SPSS Modeler http://www-01.ibm.com/software/analytics/spss/products/modeler/

(Continued)

Table 3.6 (Continued)

Package and website	Brief description
Mathematica http://www.wolfram.com/ mathematica/	A computational software program used in many scientific, engineering, mathematical, and computing fields, based on symbolic mathematics. It is an integrated system of mathematical techniques accessed by the Wolfram programming language that allows users to express problems, display results, and so on.
Mathwork's MATLAB www.mathworks.com	MATLAB (Matrix Laboratory) is a multiparadigm numerical computing environment and associated programming language intended primarily for numerical computing. Since many of the modern analytics require numerical computing, MATLAB provides a foundation for developing a rich analytical framework. It is one of the most widely used computing systems with well over a million users. It interfaces with programs written in C/C++, Java, FORTRAN, and Python.
RapidMiner https://rapidminer.com/	RapidMiner can be used as either a standalone application for data analysis or as a data mining engine for integration into an organization's systems. It provides procedures for data loading and transformation, data preprocessing, visualization, modeling, evaluation, and deployment. The Waikato Environment for Knowledge Analysis (WEKA) library is included in the package.
XLMiner http://www.solver.com/ xlminer-platform	A friendly data mining tool. The advantage of a data mining tool like XLMiner (which also has statistics functionality) is that it runs as an add-on to MS Excel, so it is convenient to further develop spreadsheet models with the analysis results.
SAP Lumira http://go.sap.com/product/ analytics/lumira.html	SAP Lumira is a data visualization software that allows users to access, transform, and visualize data. A 30-day trial version of the standard edition is available.
Tableau www.tableausoftware.com	Tableau in particular is increasing in popularity because visual analysis and presentations have strong appeal among managers.
IBM Many Eyes http://www-01.ibm.com/software/ analytics/many-eyes/	IBM's Many Eyes is a visualization package that allows users to gain insights from data without having to do extensive programming or have deep technical expertise.

Open Source Packages

There are many OSS packages that are widely used in big data processing and analysis—far too many to describe here. There are advantages and disadvantages to using OSS. Generally, the source code is available for you to download and modify if you want, but then you diverge from the main code line. The farther you diverge, the harder it becomes to maintain. Unless you actively participate in the development of open source code, you are dependent upon the community members for their vision of what the software system should be and do and their schedule for upgrades and updates.

Often, there is a lack of (good) documentation for OSS, so it can take longer to understand how it works and how to use it. Moreover, to build the infrastructure and subsystems you need for your business environment, you may have to integrate several different OSS programs together, which with the lack of documentation can take a while. Again, together, these software systems may not do exactly what you want and so your infrastructure may be a hodgepodge of pieced together software systems.

A few of the more popular OSS packages in use today are presented in Table 3.7. While these packages are largely self-contained and have large libraries associated with them, they can be difficult to use if they do not do exactly what you need.

R deserves special attention because it is a language that was specifically formulated for quantitative analysis. R is a free, open source, object-oriented programming language and it is very popular with the social science community and is becoming one of the main tools for rapid prototyping of analytics. It has surpassed commercial statistical programs in its adoption. Furthermore, all popular commercial tools like SAS and Tableau have an interface to run R within their programs. There are a number of very good reasons for this popularity, as described in Table 3.8.

Python also deserves special attention. Python is also open source, free and quite popular. But Python is a more general software language that can be used for multiple purposes like web application development, web data scraping, data manipulation and analysis, among other things. A few years back, R was considered far superior to Python for data analysis. But this has been changing rapidly in recent years because Python can be used

Table 3.7 Selected open source packages

Package and website	Brief description
Project R www.r-project.org	R is a free software environment for statistical computing and graphics. It compiles and runs on a wide variety of UNIX platforms, Windows, and MacOS. There are literally thousands of free open source R packages with just about any analytic functionality needed. There are also a wealth of development tools, integrated development environments (e.g., R Studio) and reporting tools (e.g., R Markdown, Shinny).
Python www.python.org	Python is a free software language for a multitude of programming needs (e.g., web development, data scraping), which is now replete with statistical, data management, and graphics features. It compiles and runs on a wide variety of UNIX platforms, Windows, and MacOS. There are also a wealth of development tools, integrated development environments (e.g., Spyder, Anaconda) and reporting tools (e.g., Jupyter Notebook).
WEKA http://www.cs.waikato.ac.nz/ml/weka/	WEKA is a widely used suite of machine-learning software, developed at the University of Waikato, New Zealand. It contains tools for data preprocessing, classification, regression, clustering, association rules, and visualization. It is widely used in industry, academia, and government to implement statistical machine-learning applications for data mining and predictive analytics.
Octave http://www.gnu.org/software/octave/	GNU Octave is a high-level interpreted language, primarily intended for numerical computations, including linear and nonlinear problems.
KNIME (Konstanz Information Miner) http://www.predictiveanalyticstoday.com/knime/	KNIME Desktop is a graphical workbench for data access, data transformation, predictive analytics, visualization, and reporting. KNIME uses a modular pipelining architecture to integrate multiple techniques from machine learning and data mining accessible through a graphical interface. Other variants are available for servers and clusters.
Scikit-learn http://scikit-learn.org/dev/index.html NumPy www.numpy.org SciPy http://www.scipy.org/index.html	A simple, easy-to-use tool for data mining and data analysis written in Python, a scripting language, for use in scientific analysis and programming. It incorporates NumPy and SciPy—two Python packages for numerical and scientific computing.
Spark MLlib https://spark.apache.org/mllib/	MLlib is the Spark scalable machine-learning library written in Scala. It a significant replacement for Apache Mahout which is no longer being upgraded. It runs on Hadoop, Mesos, Kubernetes, or as a standalone component as part of a Spark environment. It eliminates the limitations of MapReduce.

Table 3.8 Significant R features

R is optimized for mathematical operations, matrix algebra and statistics, which makes it ideally suited to write computational programs.
R can be used with an integrated development environment tool called R Studio, which is a very user-friendly interface that allows the analyst to work directly in the R console or in an R script, but also view things like variables, data sets, help screens, results, etc.
R is easy to learn; novice analysts begin by typing simple interactive commands into the R console, which are immediately executed and return results.
R is "vectorized," which makes it ideal to read, manipulate, and store columns of data. In addition, it has a rich set of data structures, such as: data frames (collection of column vectors, i.e., a table); and matrices (row-column structure with quantitative values); lists (collection of data of multiple types and classes).
R has literally thousands of well-documented free packages in public libraries, which users can install, activate, and use instantly with minimal programming.
R has a feature called "views," which makes it easy to install a collection of all the necessary packages for a particular type of analysis (e.g., econometrics) in one step.

for multiple purposes and it is easy to learn. Furthermore, Python is now full of popular libraries and packages for data analysis like NumPy, SciPy, Pandas, StatsModels, Matplotlib, and Scikit-learn. Furthermore, there are packages that allow Python programmers to run R code within Python like Rpy2. Python has most of the features listed for R in the table above, but it is becoming the de facto favorite for big data analytics professionals because of its vast array of features and functions beyond statistics.

CHAPTER 4

Building an Effective Big Data Organization

"The key to future success is to build an organization that can innovate with data," said Rod Morris, former senior vice-president of marketing and operations at Opower, a cloud-services firm that supplies SaaS applications to the energy and utilities industries. "To disperse the data, democratize the tools and unleash the creativity of individual employees."
—http://blogs.clicksoftware.com/clickipedia/three-steps-to-building-a-better-big-data-culture/ (no longer available)

Good organizational design and practices are essential for the success of information systems, but they are not enough. Having great technologies is also necessary for success, but they are insufficient. Having skilled personnel is key to success, but good people alone will not cut it. The key to effective information systems lies in the integration of all these three aspects. It is not only important to have great organizational practices, technology, and people, but it is also important that these three components integrate and complement each other well. This is no different for big data organizations. For example, Tom Davenport proposed these same three key elements of analytical capability—organization, human, and technology, suggesting that building an effective big data organization requires organizational practices, information technology, and talent working in harmony, just like a symphony.

In this chapter we look at some of the key components that an organization should have in place to build an enterprise-level big data program. We discussed the big data analytics (BDA) life cycle process model in

Chapter 3, but what are the key practices and structures an organization needs to succeed in its BDA efforts? We attempt to answer these questions in this chapter. Based on the many one-on-one interviews we have had with analytics professionals, countless workshops with academics and practitioners in this area, and survey studies we have conducted, we have identified these key aspects to build an effective big data organization, or to transform an organization into one. These include:

- Organizational design and practices
- People
- Talent identification and acquisition
- BDA teamwork

We discuss these key aspects in more detail in the next few sections. Before we begin, it is important to note that the shift to a service-oriented economy from a product-oriented economy has intensified over the past 20 years. Increased globalization arising from the Web and telecommunication technologies means that established markets and advanced economies must now compete with emerging economies such as India, China, and, more recently, countries in Africa. The widespread availability of and access to open source and free tools like R and big data cloud services means that any small group of individuals with great talent and education in any part of the globe can be a formidable competitor in this field. At a time in which analytic talent is so scarce, professionals in every country are waking up to this opportunity. Professionals and organizations will therefore need to be nimble and train and retrain themselves on best practices in this area to remain competitive.

A recent Bain and Company survey (Pearson and Wegener 2013) found that the use of BDA can give an organization a clear competitive advantage over its competition. An examination of more than 400 large companies found that those with the most advanced analytics were significantly outperforming their competition. These organizations were twice as likely to be in the top quartile of financial performance within their industries and were also more likely to use data very frequently when making decisions, while also making decisions faster than their competitors and much more likely successfully executing these decisions. Moreover, at the same time, the window to respond to business needs is always shrinking. Organizations should establish their organization structure for analytics and start the design and launch of a new analytics organization with a basic overall organizational architecture and approach to ensure that all of the roles, skills, and capabilities are in place from the beginning.

Organizational Design and Practices

Organizational design and management practices include a number of areas that have a significant effect on the successful use of analytics efforts within an organization. These design approaches and practices include enterprise and other architectural designs, an Analytics Body of Knowledge (AnBoK) to provide guidance to analytic practitioners, governance to help manage and ensure that the analytics efforts are aligned with business needs, and finally a culture and level of maturity that provides a positive environment for analytics success.

Enterprise, Domain, and Application Architecture

Circular A130 of the Office of Management and Budget describes enterprise architecture (EA) as "the explicit description and documentation of the current and desired relationships among business and management processes and information technology," and it provides the "blueprint" to build information systems in an organization in a coordinated manner. While it is not the objective in this chapter to promote architecture practices, we lean on EA principles to make the point that, like any other information system implementation, BDA requires careful architecting from the beginning.

The data needed for effective analytics can be either gathered from external sources or produced internally. In either case, an architecture needs to be in place to store, manage, and access this data. But data management alone is insufficient and we also need to pay attention to business processes, applications, and the technology infrastructure. Several EA frameworks have been proposed—for example, Zachman, Federal EA Framework, and The Open Group Architectural Framework—representing the various views of the architecture.

As depicted in Figure 4.1, one thing all frameworks agree on is on EA's four key players: business process, information, applications, and technology infrastructure. An organization's EA is often broken down into business domains (e.g., divisions, functions, and geographical regions), which often have their own domain architecture, and there are multiple applications running within each of these domains. In the end, all EA layers, domains, and applications must work in unison to support the organizational goals. Again, this is no different for BDA.

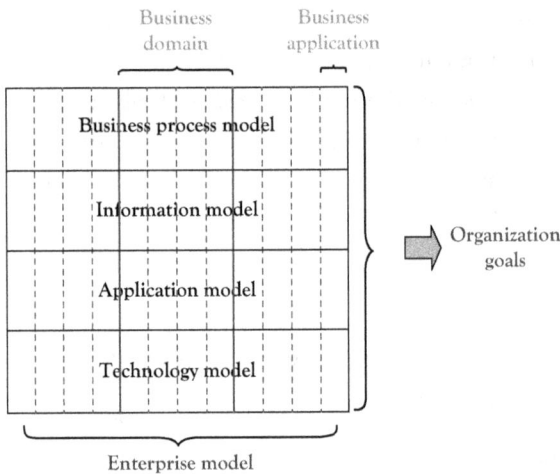

Figure 4.1 Enterprise, domain, and application architecture

The point we are trying to make is that any organization that is serious about implementing effective BDA practices needs to think way beyond talent and tools. It becomes an organizational design issue.

Business Architecture for Analytics

Business processes, whether they are enterprise, domain, or application processes, need to incorporate big data and analytic thinking into them. It was sufficient in the past to conceptualize business processes to fulfill the transactional needs of the organization, but this is no longer the case. For example, some of the most advanced Internet marketing analytics practices collect terabytes of data, gathering all the customer shopping and clicking behavior online, which can later be mined to develop customized marketing strategies. However, the necessary business processes to gather, store, retrieve, and analyze the necessary data must be in place.

Furthermore, business processes are just about everywhere. The collection of "key process indicators" of process performance is now taking place at a very granular level and in just about all process steps. For example, when you order food at a restaurant, it is not uncommon to track the time it takes from seating to ordering, from ordering to kitchen preparation, from preparation to serving, from serving to ordering the bill and then to paying the bill. Thousands of these process timestamps and counts provide rich insights into business process efficiencies.

Business Architecture (BA) Aligns Analytics Initiatives and Business Outcomes

Without a BA, analytics efforts are, in many cases, not aligned to the business objectives, and thus fail to meet user expectations. The overall enterprise architecture should include analytics architectural components, prioritized initiatives, and their relationship to business needs. Thus, the business needs drive the analytics efforts. An analytics governance process helps to maintain this critical alignment.

The same is true for the information model. Many online shopping sites were not interested in collecting shopping cart data in the early years and most of this data was stored locally in cookies in the users' computers. All the companies need was to be able to move shopping cart contents to the checkout application to process the sale transaction. Not anymore; today, companies are tracking all aspects of shopping cart behavior (e.g., the timing when items are added, modified, or deleted; the elapsed time between a shopping cart addition and a product purchase; the likelihood of purchasing once a product is added to the shopping cart; the amount of time a buyer spends in the product specifications before buying; the most effective colors and graphics to motivate a buyer to make a purchase, etc.).

The application architecture also needs to be designed with BDA in mind. If the analysis is done by humans, maybe all that is necessary is to have applications that produce the necessary data and the tools to analyze it. But more progressive organizations do analytics on the fly as the data arrives. An online shopping application that makes product recommendations based on social filtering (i.e., "people like you who bought this item also bought this other item") cannot afford to wait for human intervention to make these recommendations, so they embed analytic applications within their transactional systems.

Finally, the technology architecture to support BDA has to be in place. An organization committed to collecting lots of data for analytics must have the necessary infrastructure to manage this data effectively. Again, if the analysis is done by humans, perhaps all that is needed is large data storage capacity and data warehousing facilities, where the data can be easily accessed and downloaded for analysis. If the data needs to be analyzed in real time, then the organization will need to invest in big data facilities so that the analysis can be run directly in the big data environment.

Analytics Body of Knowledge Focus

While it is common knowledge that analytical talent is in high demand and short supply, the necessary knowledge to do effective analytic work is not just confined to the analytic and quantitative domains. Functional domain knowledge is also necessary to do effective analytical work. It is important to note that some organizations are reporting that the number of years of experience to become an expert in a knowledge domain (e.g., financial analysis) is dramatically shrinking, because younger, less experienced analysts can access the data and derive similar intelligence from the data faster than a former domain expert without the data analysis skills can. Nevertheless, decisions cannot be made in a vacuum and, given that analytics permeates all aspects of organizational work, it is necessary for analysts to have some degree of functional domain knowledge. In order to better understand the knowledge that analytics professionals need to possess, we developed a body of knowledge framework for analytics (AnBoK). We have used this body of knowledge successfully to analyze the educational market in BDA and design a Master's of Science degree program based on it.

Implementing a successful organizational analytics program can be a challenging set of activities. When we speak of a holistic approach to

BDA within an organization, there are knowledge areas to address when implementing the program. We developed our AnBoK, illustrated in Figure 4.2, from information gathered from numerous interviews, workshops, roundtables, conference discussions, surveys, and interviews of analytics professionals and academics. This framework is composed of four layers: foundations, analytics core, functional domains, and management. We now discuss each of these in more detail.

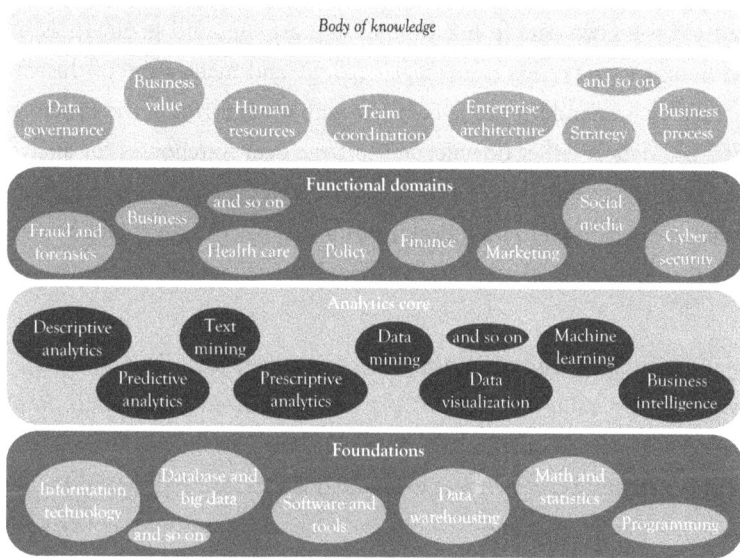

Figure 4.2 Analytics body of knowledge

Foundations Layer

These are the basic skills and infrastructure needed to operate and support a robust organizational analytics program. BDA is at the intersection of several disciplines, including computer science, software programming, database querying, mathematics, statistics, operations research, management science, and information systems, among others. These are many of the core information technology tools and infrastructure discussed in Volume II. While a full discussion of the basic foundations of analytics is beyond the scope of this chapter, we highlight important foundations.

Database, Big Data, and Data Warehousing.   The analytics team will need access to the data as large amounts of raw data may exist in a multitude of formats: structured (relational) and unstructured (tweets, Web blogs, text documents, etc.). For structured data management, knowledge of tools and data platforms is necessary to manage high-volume structured data (for instance, clickstream data or machine/sensor data). For unstructured data management, there is a focus on managing the explosion in data volumes due, to a large extent, to sources such as social media, Web transaction data, RFID and other sensor data, videos, pictures, machine generated and even text data from customer support logs, and so on. Tools and technologies are needed to manage, analyze, and make sense of this data to build understanding and to correlate with other forms of the structured data. Big data is either downloaded to large data warehouses for analysis (i.e., traditional analytics) or analyzed directly in the big data environment. Either way, any organization dealing with the five Vs of big data needs to have the talent to work with and analyze data in these environments.

Information Technology, Software, Programming, and Tools.   To effectively capture value from BDA, organizations need to integrate information technology, software, and programming tools into the analytics architecture and process. These technology decisions need careful analysis since they can have a long-term impact on an organization's ability to integrate BDA, as well as inform what skills need to be developed and how they are best developed. In many cases, pilots and prototyping initiatives are needed to test out and experiment with new tools and architectures.

Mathematics and Statistics.   The organization will need individuals that have foundational skills in statistics and advanced mathematics. To be able to perform advanced analytics on big data, the analyst will need to understand such statistical concepts as correlation and multivariate regression, as well as be able to model and view data from different perspectives for use in predictive and prescriptive modeling.

Software and Tools.   As we mentioned earlier, big data can be harvested from a variety of sources. Organizations need to identify and deploy tools to gather, process, and visualize the information in useful and effective ways. Technologies include high-capacity storage repositories, modern databases, and specialized applications that can be used to reduce and consolidate big data, as well as find patterns and make sense of the data. Compounding these challenges, the analytics technology tools space is rapidly changing. New tools and software are being introduced at a rapid rate. Choices need to be made based on analytics. Organizations need to address some key technology decisions, including the following:

- Which technologies and tools are needed to support our analytics architecture based on our business goals and objectives?
- Which platforms are best suited to integrating these new tools, as well as work with any existing technologies?
- Are open source or proprietary solutions the right fit for our organization?

An organization's analysts may need access to advanced analytical tools, such as Hadoop, NoSQL, SAS and so on, as well as programming skills, particularly in languages such as R and Python. Regardless of the specific technologies chosen, a critical component of the AnBoK is the ability to manipulate data using software, so the need for skilled programmers will not go away. For example, given that big data may come from a variety of sources and in a variety of formats, merging structured and unstructured big data requires specialized and advanced knowledge, and tools and technologies to prepare the data for analysis in analytical models.

Technologies such as in-database and in-memory analytics provide capabilities to process large data sets for analysis at near real-time speeds and to combine the analytics environment within, for example, structured data management tools. Additionally, an organization will need to develop an approach for master data management and consistently support an analytics culture at all levels of the organization.

Finally, the representation of data and results are an important component of big data architecture. Visualization tools allow the analysis to be more clearly understood and insights to be discovered. Visualization tools and technologies for quick drill down and analysis are now available and need to be integrated into analytics architectures, like the one illustrated in Figure 4.3. Finally, the organization will need to address how to integrate these analytic technologies to provide value to the organization, by aligning to and supporting the business decision-making process.

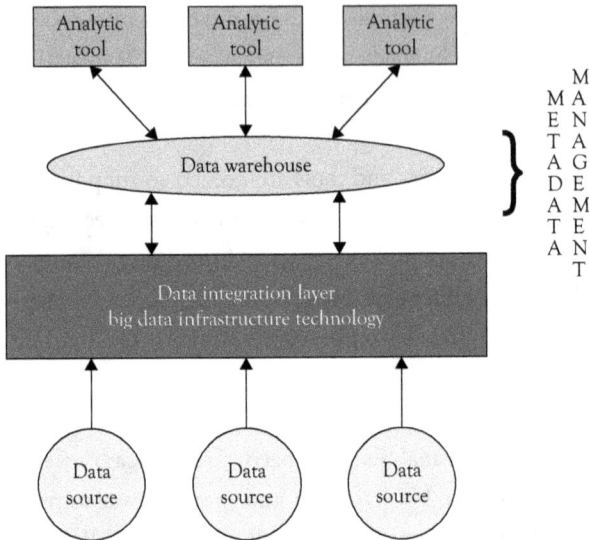

Figure 4.3 Logical analytics integration architecture

Analytics Core

These are the disciplines that often come to mind when we read or hear about BDA and it includes the typical topics found in most analytics books, like descriptive analytics, predictive analytics, machine learning, data mining, and business intelligence, among others. As discussed in Chapter 3, analytics approaches can be partitioned into three broad areas: descriptive, predictive, and prescriptive. The integrated role that these approaches play in organization analytics approach is outlined in Table 4.1.

Functional Domains

Analytics is never performed in isolation, but in the context of a specific functional domain like health care, marketing, finance, policy analysis, fraud detection, accounting forensics, cyber security analysis, and sustainability, among many others. Just about every discipline can benefit

Table 4.1 The role various analytics play in data-driven decision making

Past and present—descriptive analytics	The future—predictive and prescriptive analytics
Create awareness and determine that a decision needs to be made	Identify likely outcomes—predictive—ever increasing sophistication in machine learning methods
Report on the results of action	Identify the best course of action—prescriptive
Understand the scope and context of the decision	Develop explanatory capabilities that "walkback" through the provenance of the analysis

from analytics. So the basic question is: What makes the best analyst? Is it a data scientist who develops some knowledge of a given functional domain through experience? Or is it a functional worker (e.g., investment broker) who gets additional education in analytics? We argue that functional professionals with a deep understanding of and expertise in their domains make the best analysts because they have a stronger foundation to formulate analytics questions and interpret and explain results.

Management

To be successful at the organizational level, the analytics efforts must be appropriately supported by management functions and processes. Analytics efforts are not likely to yield results of strategic value if the organization's long-term strategy is not aligned with analytics. Similarly, no analytics project will be successful unless the various component activities are appropriately coordinated and staffed.

Finding analytics talent is difficult these days, so human resources plays a critical role. It is not uncommon to hear complaints from Chief Information Officers (CIOs) that they need to pay very high salaries for analytic talent, who end up leaving the firm before one year has elapsed. In big data and data science, it is often the case that the grass is usually greener in the next field. Management must have an active retention strategy to ensure that its best people stay engaged, compensated, and trained in the latest techniques.

Data governance is another key issue. Data is the most valuable asset in modern organizations today, beyond their personnel. No insurance policy that we have heard of provides coverage for data losses. Hence, all aspects of data ownership, sharing, access, security, and location need to be covered by governance policies.

Governance

BDA governance can be thought of as the approach that analytics-based organizations use to define, prioritize, and track analytic initiatives as well as to manage different types and categories of data related to analytics. According to Gartner, less than "10% of self-service BI initiatives will be governed sufficiently to prevent inconsistencies that adversely affect the business" (Oestreich and Tapadinhas 2018). BDA governance strives to ensure that organizations have reliable and consistent data to perform analytics and make management decisions. Particularly with the decentralized use of analytic capabilities across business, there is a need for consistency and transparency, because:

- The significant increase in available internal and external data sources increases the risk of illegitimate and unethical application of analytics, and
- Organizations need to understand the related impacts and establish new rules and policies when business decisions are automated and performed by smart machines and machine-learning algorithms.

Without a corporate-wide BDA governance framework in place, the risks an organization faces include, but are not limited to:

- Missing opportunities due to incorrect or insufficient utilization of analytics
- Damage to the organizations' reputation due to illegal or unethical application of analytics (e.g., privacy and security)
- Making bad decisions based on analytics and data that is not often fully understood by the decision makers
- Understanding the implications of specific automated decision making based on analytic results

- The legal and economic consequences of not complying with regulatory requirements
- Finally, cost or quality issues due to misalignment of analytical-based performance measurement across the organization

Thoughtful and appropriate governance helps to encourage actions in support of business objectives and prevent unnecessary efforts. General governance attributes include defining and assigning decision rights within the organization (e.g., with senior management or within areas of competency, ensuring that analytics efforts are aligned with business objectives and processes). Determining the priority alignment of analytical initiatives to business objectives and processes requires both portfolio management and governance. The governance approach should be documented and communicated with analytic big data policies and procedures; for analytic initiatives, measures should be defined to ensure and track the effort and the accomplishment of a business goal or decision.

Key tasks in implementing BDA governance include:

- Delegating analytics authority, budget, and responsibility to the appropriate unit or department
- Defining and taking responsibility for the corporate analytics metrics framework and then ensuring alignment with the business' goals and strategy
- Reviewing, prioritizing, and selecting BDA initiatives and deciding on corporate level investment budget for BDA
- Tracking and enforcing metrics and indicators to assess return on big data investments
- Developing performance indicators to identify policy, compliance, and regulatory adherence
- Ensuring the integration of analytics governance with information governance and within the broader business and IT governance processes.

In starting to build an analytics governance framework, consider the goals and objectives for the various forms and types of big data initiatives shown, for example, in Table 4.2.

Table 4.2 Big data initiatives type

Information portal	Business analytics	Analytics laboratory	Operational
Descriptive	Descriptive	Predictive	Prescription
Focus on data models and information governance aspects	Focus on analytic models and business analyst self-service	Focus on prediction models	Focus on decision models and integration in business processes
Efficiency Integrity Security	Consistency Alignment Relevance	Transparency Privacy Quality	Viability Fidelity Appropriateness

Big Data Analytics Culture

In implementing a successful analytics program, organizations need to broadly focus on a number of key analytical and technology practices and be business-centric rather than IT-centric. Organizations need to plan and quickly adapt to changing roles and skill sets, and they need to balance business and IT skills and resources, while building partnerships between the business stakeholders and the information technology group. With the core technology and skills in place throughout the organization, the organization needs to institutionalize the importance and value of data-driven decision making to the company at large. A culture that embraces data and facts and applies them to everyday business should be grown. The challenge requires both top-down and bottom-up approaches to ensure that everyone gets on board with the new data-driven paradigm.

When the organization has institutionalized the management, skills, tools, and technology necessary to drive an analytics-based organization, they will be prepared to innovate with the big data and continually find new ways to leverage their big data analytical abilities. Data-driven organizations need to value analytics as much as instinct when making decisions, and they need to view information as an asset and understand how to measure and communicate the value of BDA to all their stakeholders. The organization's culture should grow and change as people use the technology to take informed actions. When taking an organization-wide approach to analytics, key technology practices should be implemented, including developing and executing an EA strategy, and working to prevent or eliminate silos of capability, as well as implementing an integrated analytics toolset and delivery platform.

Big Data Analytics Maturity

As the field of BDA matures, frameworks will emerge to evaluate the analytic maturity of organizations. The Software Engineering Institute developed the infamous *Capability Maturity Model* (CMM) establishing five levels of software organization maturity based on whether the company employed certain key processes needed to build software effectively and efficiently with repeatable patterns of success. Today, the CMM is the de facto standard of software maturity.

Similarly, Jeanne Ross and colleagues developed a four-level CMM for EA, starting with stove-piped silos at level 1, all the way to a modular architecture at level 4. CMMs are very good because they help gauge the level of sophistication and reliability that organizations have in the particular domain the model is designed to measure. For example, bids for contracts often require the software companies to be at CMM levels 4 or 5 (Ross, Weill, and Robertson 2006, p. 69).

Recently, several maturity models for big data have been developed and have been adopted by multiple organizations. Tom Davenport (2007) proposed five stages of development for analytics capabilities as depicted in Table 4.3.

Table 4.3 Five stages of analytic capabilities

Stage	Description
Prerequisites to analytical capabilities	A good transaction data environment and operations exist.
Prove-it detour	Most organizations progress to stage two directly, but some need this detour to prove their analytical capabilities.
Analytical aspirations	This stage occurs when analytics gains executive support and first major analytics projects are launched.
Analytical company	This stage is achieved when the organization has demonstrated world-class analytical capabilities at the enterprise level.
Analytical competitors	This stage occurs when analytics go beyond being a capability to becoming strategic for competitive advantage.

Niall Betteridge, of IBM Australia, developed an initial analytics maturity model based on six capability categories having five levels of maturity which are described in Tables 4.4 and 4.5.

Table 4.4 Analytics capability categories (adapted from Nott 2015)

Analytics capability	Description
Business strategy	The business strategy and associated business expertise are necessary to develop meaningful insights and distinguish among different outcomes. An organization must be able to explore data for new opportunities and construct quantified business cases to innovate and create new business models.
Information	Information is the major business asset of a modern business organization. It comes from multiple systems—both internal and external—and must be integrated to provide decision-making utility. Mature organization have established governance practices to ensure access, accuracy, and reliability of derived data.
Analytics	Analytics are necessary to understand what has happened, why it happened, and predict what will happen next. Insights generated by analytics will support data-driven decision making to improve business operations efficiency.
Cultural and operation execution	Access to data and analytics usage yield no business value in and of itself. Rather, when people apply the insights obtained, they can visualize, share, and provide feedback to improve business operations. Mature organizations ensure that data and analytics services are aligned to and evolve with business priorities.
Architecture	An overall technology and data management approach is essential to ensuring access to data, deployment of analytic services, and analytic and decision-making support to end users and business operations. A mature organization uses architecture to ensure the five Vs support through architectural patterns, standards, service level agreements, and security to analytics services.
Governance	Governance is necessary to ensure confidence in the reliability, accuracy, and maintenance of data across an organization and the insights derived from analytic processing. Governance requires policies for provenance, master data and metadata management, data quality, security, privacy, and ethical use.

Table 4.5 *Analytics maturity model (adapted from Nott 2015)*

Business strategy	Big data is discussed but not reflected in business strategy, in which use of data extends simply to financial and regulatory reporting.	The business strategy recognizes that data can be used to generate business value and return on investment (ROI), though realization is largely experimental.	The business strategy encourages the use of insight from data within business processes.	The business strategy realizes the competitive advantage of using client-centric insight.	Data drives continuous business model innovation.
Information	The organization uses its historical structured data to observe its business.	Information is used to effectively manage the business.	Information is applied to improve operational processes and client engagement.	Relevant information in context is used as a differentiator.	Information is used as a strategic asset.
Analytics	Analytics is limited to describing what has happened.	Analytics is used to inform decision makers why something in the business has happened.	Analytical insight is used to predict the likelihood of what will happen to some current business activity.	Predictive analytics is used to help optimize an organization's decision making so that the best actions are taken to maximize business value.	Analytical insight optimizes business processes and is automated where possible.
Culture and operational execution	The application of analytical insight is the choice of the individual and has little effect on how the organization operates.	The organization understands the causes behind observations in business processes, but its culture is largely resistant to adaptation that takes advantage of the insight.	The organization makes limited business decisions using analytical insight to improve operational efficiency and generate additional value.	Decision makers are well informed with insight from analytics, and the organization is capable of acting to maximize resulting business value.	The organization and its business processes continuously adapt and improve using analytical insight in line with strategic business objectives.

(continued)

Table 4.5 (Continued)

Architecture	The organization does not have a single, coherent information architecture.	An information architecture framework exists but does not extend to new data sources or advanced analytics capabilities.	Best-practice information architectural patterns for big data and analytics are defined and have been applied in certain areas.	Information architecture and associated standards are well defined and cover most of the volume, variety, velocity, and veracity capabilities and structured and unstructured data consumption needed for differentiation.	Information architecture fully underpins business strategies to enable complete market disruption with volume, variety, velocity, and veracity specifications applied.
Governance	Information governance is largely manual and barely sufficient to stand up to legal, audit, and other regulatory scrutiny.	Understanding of data and its ownership are defined and managed in a piecemeal fashion.	Policies and procedures are implemented to manage and protect core information through its life in the organization.	The degree of confidence in information and resulting insights is reflected in making decisions.	Information governance is integrated into all aspects of the business processes.

People

As with most endeavors in life, people are perhaps the most critical aspect for the success of an analytics-based organization. While roles and skills will vary depending on the organization (e.g., size, business domain, specific needs etc.), a number of key roles and related skills needed in big data analytical organizations are highlighted in Table 4.6. Often, a single individual will fulfill several of these roles as the duties and responsibilities are combined under one title.

Table 4.6 Key big data team roles

Role	Description
Chief Data Officer/ Chief Information Officer	The Chief Data Officer (CDO) is a senior executive who bears responsibility for the firm's enterprise-wide data and information strategy and governance. The Chief Information Officer (CIO) is responsible for all of the information processing resources and systems within an organization.
Chief Knowledge Officer	The Chief Knowledge Officer (CKO) is responsible for the intellectual capital and knowledge management practices and procedures within the organization.
Chief Analytics Officer	The Chief Analytics Officer (CAO) is the senior manager responsible for the analysis of data within an organization.
Chief Portfolio Integration Manager	The Chief Portfolio Integration Manager (CPIM) is the senior manager responsible for ensuring the integration of services and applications that deliver value to the decision-making operations of the organization—whether internal or external.
Analytically informed business managers	All managers and business analysts need to understand and have an appreciation for what analytics can and cannot do.
Data analyst	A data analyst's job is to capture business requirements, analyze, and model supporting data and use it to help companies make better business decisions.
Data scientist	Data scientists are analytical data experts who have the technical skills to solve complex, analytical problems.
Big data technologist	The big data technologist architects, implements, and administers the BDA technology and tools within the big data ecosystem.

Chief Data Officer/Chief Information Officer

While typically not formally on the analytics team, the *Chief Data Officer* (CDO) plays a critical role in ensuring that the data needed by the analytics team is available, accurate, consistent, and reliable. The CDO is a senior executive who bears responsibility for the firm's enterprise-wide data and information strategy and governance.

The CDO's role will combine accountability and responsibility for information protection and privacy, information governance and information, data quality, and data life cycle management, along with the exploitation of data assets to create business value.

The *Chief Information Officer* (CIO) is often a member of the executive management team of an organization and is responsible for all information-processing resources and systems within the organization.

Chief Knowledge Officer

The *Chief Knowledge Officer* (CKO) is responsible for the intellectual capital of an organization and oversees the knowledge management process within the organization. This role may have significant legal responsibilities such as managing the patent portfolio and information and technology exchange agreements with other organizations.

Chief Analytic Officer

While the CDO is responsible for the collection, storage, and management of data, the *Chief Analytics Officer* (CAO) focuses on providing input into operational decisions on the basis of the analysis. The CAO is the senior manager responsible for the analysis of data within an organization. The CAO addresses creating real business value through data analytics and promoting the organization's data-driven culture. As such, the CAO requires experience in statistical analysis and marketing, finance, or operations. The CAO oversees the organization's overall analytic approach and helps to ensure that the analytic efforts are prioritized at the strategic level and that the analytic initiatives align with business goals and objectives, with the analytic results informing business decision makers.

Chief Portfolio Integration Manager

The *Chief Portfolio Integration Manager* (CPIM) is responsible for the end-to-end success of the application portfolio that delivers decision-making support for business operations to internal and external clients within an organization. The CPIM is the single point of consolidation and integration of services developed across the organization. He develops the strategy and implementation plan, ensures alignment of services to business operations, and determines when new services are required to provide new functionality or when to replace old services.

Analytically Informed Business Managers

While it is not reasonable, nor desirable, in most cases, that the vast majority of business managers and analysts are deeply trained in the knowledge of analytics, it is very important that they need to learn how to analyze data and become a savvy consumer of analytics information. Managers and business analysts need to understand and have an appreciation for what analytics can and cannot do, as well as know how to identify business needs that can be addressed with analytics and communicate these business needs to the analytics team.

Data Analyst

The *data analyst's* job is to capture business requirements, analyze and model supporting data, and use it to help companies make better business decisions. The data analyst will be responsible for gathering, modeling, analyzing, and reporting data from a wide range of sources. Data analysts will need the business knowledge to understand the business problem and determine what data is needed to model the problem. They also need knowledge of statistical and analytical techniques to be able to analyze the data, as well as business insight to be able to interpret analysis results in business terms.

Data Scientist

Data scientists are analytical experts who have the technical skills to solve complex, analytical problems utilizing, in many cases, advanced statistics, math, and programming languages. They are part mathematician, part computer scientist, and part analyst, and, often, part database designer and visualization scientist as well.

They normally have a strong foundation in such disciplines as computer science and applications, modeling, statistics, analytics, and math. Data scientists have advanced training in multivariate statistics, artificial intelligence, machine learning, mathematical programming, and simulation to perform descriptive, predictive, and prescriptive analytics. Data scientists often hold PhD degrees. Big data organizations typically will need to augment existing analytical staff with data scientists, who will have a higher level of technical capabilities, as well as the ability to manipulate big data technologies. These capabilities might include natural language processing and text mining skills, and experience with video and image manipulation. Data scientists also have the ability to code in scripting languages such as Python, Pig, and Hive.

Big Data Technologist—Infrastructure and Tools

The *big data technologist* architects, implements, and administers the BDA technology and tools within the big data ecosystem. These technologies vary, but can include the Hadoop ecosystem, MapReduce, Spark, databases (both NOSQL and SQL), in-memory databases, data warehouses/lakes, analytical modeling and visualization tools, and so on. Those in this role can also be responsible for the extracting, transforming, and loading of data from various source systems into the analytical platform/data staging areas.

Talent Identification and Acquisition—Staffing the Analytics Operation

Many large organizations already have data analysts even if they do not have a formal BDA program. As you start a BDA program, you must consider where to obtain the skilled resources to staff it. Five primary means for obtaining skilled team members are: (1) hiring trained data and analytics scientists, (2) developing an in-house training program, (3) partnering with a college/university to provide a formal training program, (4) utilizing commercial educational programs, and (5) contracting out the BDA function. Each approach has its advantages and disadvantages.

Most importantly, an organization needs people who have the skills in the analytic techniques and methods that best address the business problems and operations within the organization.

Hiring Trained Staff

This is one of the quickest ways to organize and staff a BDA program. The number of trained and skilled data and analytic scientists has increased, as many data science and data analytics programs have come online through college and university programs. These programs are increasing and are starting to provide a large pool of potential employees. But, this pool will not be sufficient to satisfy the projected demand for skilled analytical professions given by the Department of Labor. Of course, we understand that you cannot wait and must have a BDA staff right now.

Harris, Murphy, and Vaisman (2013) analyzed corporate requirements for BDA staff and the corresponding skills of people who billed themselves as "data scientists." They found that many employers have unrealistic expectations of potential staff. Harris et al. called this the "rock star syndrome" or the desire to have one person who can do it all—the *Data Creatives*. These individuals can do it all: extract data, integrate it, create compelling visualization mechanisms, perform statistical and analytical analyses, and build the necessary tools when good ones do not exist. Good luck with that! These people are rare and are most likely hackers rather than disciplined practitioners.

Harris et al. identified three other categories of data scientists. The *Data Business people* are focused on the organization and how data projects can yield profits or provide better services to clients. Most have a technical undergraduate degree and an advanced degree (such as an MBA), are highly disciplined in their approach, and have experience in contracting or consulting work. Another group is the *Data Developers*, who are usually focused on managing the data—preparing it, organizing it, transforming it, and storing it. They do not necessarily analyze it as much as make it ready for analysis or derive data that can be used in analysis. The final group is the *Data Researchers*, who generally have deep academic training—PhDs and technical publications. They are focused on developing new methods of analysis to understand complex processes in business or other fields.

So, which ones do you need, or put another way, how do you build a staff given these categories of data scientists? It depends on what you are trying to do. Our suggestion is to start off with a few people from the "Data Business people" and a few from the "Data Developers." This provides you with a staff to manage your data and a staff to begin developing solutions to benefit the business operations and decision making. As your organization gains experience with BDA, you can move into more complex business and technical decision processes and you can add a few "Data Researchers" to develop advanced and alternative analytical techniques. Finally, to handle ad hoc, critical problems, you may decide to hire one or two people from the "Data Creatives" category. (Note: We have termed these individuals *Analytic Scientists* in Kaisler, Armour, Espinosa, and Money 2014)

Communication, Organizational Skills, and Knowledge

We have discussed and will continue to discuss in this chapter the need for individuals who have a sound foundation of skills that include analytical and big data modeling, tools, and technology. However, while some analytical personnel will focus narrowly on specific big data and analytics approaches, there will be a need for more broad-based individuals who match technical data knowledge with great business, communication, and presentation skills.

Analytics teams should have the capability to identify unexpected and critical analytical insights via an understanding of business needs. The analytics professional also needs to be able to effectively converse in the language of business with the users to determine the best analytical approaches to address the specific business user's requirements. Additionally, they must be able to explain and communicate these insights to the business users and executives.

In Walmart (Marr 2015), for example, analytics and big data are now integrated into every vertical element within the company. Every new analytics team member participates in the Walmart Analytics Rotation Program and spends time in different business departments to understand how they operate and how analytics can be used across the various organizations. We discuss typical analytics organizational structures later in this chapter.

INFORMS (https://www.informs.org/Community/Analytics), a professional society that focuses on promoting the use of data-driven analytics and fact-based decision making in practice, has an analytics certification called Certified Analytics Professional (CAP). When creating the CAP, INFORMS (Nestler et al. 2012) discussed "T" shaped analytics knowledge vs. "I" shaped knowledge. A person with "T" expertise understands, at a high level, a wide breadth of knowledge surrounding their discipline, with in-depth knowledge of one or more narrower areas, whereas a person with "I" shaped expertise tends to focus exclusively on narrower, but a deeper set of skills. Organizations should be careful to staff their analytics program with a mix of individuals with both "T" and "I" shaped expertise.

The INFORMS CAP certification requires, among other things, passing a certification test, having at least a BA/BS degree, multiple years of analytical work experience, and being effective using soft skills. For more information on the INFORMS CAP, see www.certifiedanalytics.org.

In-House Training

Another approach, which will take some time, is to develop an in-house training program. One advantage is that you can select people with the apparent aptitude and background, who may already be business analysts and have considerable business domain knowledge, to enhance their skills and capabilities and value to the organization. Most often, an organization will contract an external organization to train their people in a select set of skills directly relevant to its immediate business needs.

At a recent roundtable of C-level executives (Private Sector IT Assembly 2015, Panel on Global Enterprise, Big Data Trends, Analytics and Insights), one experienced panelist expressed concerns about the difficulty of attracting highly trained and qualified data scientists. The observation this colleague made was that these data scientists came at a very high price tag and often did not last more than one year with the organization. Data scientists are in very high demand these days and they are very difficult to pin down. The same colleague indicated that their organization (a very large consulting firm) had more success training in-house personnel.

Unless an employee has been highly educated in both analytics and a functional domain, it is likely that they will only have expertise in one or the other. Hence, one approach is to train quantitative and technical staff in the specific functional domains of interest. Another approach is to train managers and functional domain experts in BDA. This panelist indicated that the best analytics person they had was a functional domain employee who had some basic foundation of statistics, who became a leading analyst after receiving the necessary training.

In either case, the organization should create and maintain a retention program which includes a continuous training component to allow in-house personnel to expand and enhance their skills. An aspect of this might be to require every analytic staff member to acquire at least one new skill per year as part of their job. A few studies have shown that continuous investment in technical personnel is a strong factor in retention.

College and University Education Programs

This approach takes an academic approach to developing a BDA capability by allowing existing staff to become "credentialed" by earning a certificate or Master's degree in big data. At the same time, it provides an organization with a conduit for examining and hiring current and graduating students to build a BDA staff. Two advantages of this approach are that it can provide a pipeline for future hires and access to professors with expertise in a variety of domains and analytic disciplines.

Because of the widespread belief that there is an ever-widening gap between supply and demand of both deep analytical data scientists and managers with analytical skills, schools have embarked in a gold-rush-like race to create appealing degrees in data science, analytics, and big data. One thing that is important to note is that BDA and traditional analytics can be classified as STEM programs. STEM stands for Science, Technology, Engineering, and Math, and there is a big national push to increase STEM education in the United States. Furthermore, international students enrolled in STEM education programs can get an additional 17 months of practical training visas. We strongly encourage readers with an interest in analytics education to seek STEM-approved programs.

For more information visit: http://www.dhs.gov/news/2012/05/11/ dhs-announces-expanded- list-stem-degree-programs.

With the help of an external consulting organization, American University conducted a comprehensive study of about 40 different programs in big data and analytics. Our conclusion is that there is a rapid growth of educational programs catering to this market, and those seeking further college education in this area need to be careful about the programs they select. (See https://onlinebusiness.american.edu/analytics/)

George Washington University, in creating its Master's Program in Data Analytics, surveyed the offerings of a number of colleges and universities, some for-profit organizations, and major organizations in the Washington, DC metropolitan area. From these inputs, it created a two-year program that provides five foundational courses and optional courses that allow a student to orient his or her interest in analytics towards different areas. (See https://programs.gwu.edu/data-analytics)

We see a lot of confusion among applicants, which is not unexpected, given the fact that BDA is still an emerging field. In our attempt to make some sense out of the jungle of possibilities for education in analytics, we classified big data and analytics programs using our AnBoK framework into the categories presented in Table 4.7.

Numerous programs exist in business analytics. American University's program in the Kogod School of Business is an exemplar of the type of business analytics program that will evolve in the future. American University has implemented a novel one-year Master of Science in Analytics by partnering with various departments in the business school and other schools across campus. The program includes 9 credits of foundational courses, 9 credits of analytics core courses, and 12 credits of functional specialization courses from the various departments and schools participating in the degree. For example, if a student wishes to specialize in accounting forensics analytics, they can take the required foundational and core analytic courses and combine that with 12 credits of accounting forensics courses. In addition, the program has a capstone practicum in which students work on a real project with real data, and no lectures.

George Washington University (GWU) has implemented a new Master's program in Data Analytics that is jointly managed by the School of Engineering and Applied Science (SEAS) and the Business School. Students take five core courses and then can choose a track from either SEAS

Table 4.7 Big data and analytics programs

Category	Description
Data science programs	These programs center around the first two layers of the AnBoK. Their focus is on developing fundamental skills in quantitative sciences and statistics, followed by a solid foundation of topics in the analytics core layer. It is doubtful that any school can really prepare a true data scientist in a short one-year program. Data scientists often have doctoral degrees in quantitative fields; they are in very short supply and in high demand.
Analytics programs	These programs differ in key aspects from traditional data science programs. Like with data science programs, they focus on the first two layers of the AnBoK framework, but the coursework focuses more on analytics than big data, whereas data science tends to go deeper into big data topics.
Business analytics programs	While this may seem to be a subtle semantic differentiation, the market appears to be viewing "analytics" programs as deeply analytical and "business analytics" programs as ones that aim to support functional domains, focusing on managers that need analytical skills and consumers of analytics reports. As such, these programs focus on the first three layers of the AnBoK—foundational, analytics core, and functional domain. For example, some schools have very effective programs specializing in specific functional areas, like marketing analytics, health care analytics, and cybersecurity analytics, among others.
Analytics programs— highly technical and foundational programs	These programs focus on education around the foundational layer of the AnBoK. These programs are typically found in computer science or mathematics schools. They tend to focus on basic mathematics, statistics, quantitative analysis, software programming, and computing infrastructures.
Tool-based programs	These programs focus on providing students the skills to use popular analytics and business intelligence tools like RapidMiner, XLMiner, and Tableau, among others. These are typically short certification programs and we caution the reader to study these programs carefully. A power tool in the hands of a novice can do more damage than good and we encourage readers to look into more foundational programs.
Theoretical vs. practical approaches	Some schools focus on teaching students the fundamentals and theories associated with BDA, whereas others follow a more practical approach. In our experience, we find that students trained with ample opportunities to put into practice what they have learned—through practicums or internships—become the most effective analysts who are ready to hit the ground running upon graduation. We call this "experiential learning."

or the Business School. Students are required to complete a capstone project in the final term of their Master's program. The Columbia College of Arts and Sciences (CCAS) has also instituted a Master's program in Data Science with several required courses and an array of alternatives for completing the program.

Commercial Education Opportunities

Commercial training organizations, tool vendors, and open source organizations provide many possible training opportunities. The list is endless and is evolving very quickly. Table 4.8 lists a few commercial education opportunities or training sites that provide big data training options. We should caution you to thoroughly investigate the backgrounds of the teachers and lecturers in a commercial firm before committing to them to educate your staff.

Table 4.8 Selected commercial training opportunities

Commercial training	Description
Teradata University Network (www.teradatauniversitynetwork.com)	Free, web-based portal that provides teaching and learning tools. The resources and content support everything from introduction to IT at the undergraduate level to graduate- and executive-level courses in big data and analytics.
Big Data University (http://bigdatauniversity.com/)	Online courses on big data topics, that are mostly free, developed by experienced professionals and teachers.
Lynda (www.lynda.com)	A wide selection of online videos on a multitude of topics including, but not limited to, big data and analytic methods and tools.
SAS (https://support.sas.com/training/)	Provides a variety of training courses on SAS software and associated analytics skills.
Hortonworks (http://hortonworks.com/training/)	Provides training designed by Hadoop experts. Scenario-based training courses are available in-classroom or online.
EMC (https://education.emc.com/guest/campaign/data_science.aspx	Curriculum-based training and approach to the techniques and tools required for BDA.

Outsourcing the Big Data Analytics Function

The final approach is to contract out the BDA capability to a third-party firm already established in BDA. This approach is usually more expensive, but can often be implemented relatively quickly. It allows the BDA staff to grow and/or shrink as the organization's need varies. Moreover, it can often provide a quicker route to introduce new analytic techniques into the BDA process.

Big Data Analytics Teamwork

> The sexy job in the next ten years will be statisticians . . . The ability to take data—to be able to understand it, to process it, to extract value from it, to visualize it, to communicate it—that's going to be a hugely important skill. (Varian, *Mckinsey Quarterly*, 2009)

The analytics teams will oversee the design, building, testing, and deployment of analytical models, reports, and data visual representations. Creating a successful analytics team requires both the right people and the right culture. Applying BDA within an organization is not a solitary process. While data and analytic scientists may work on individual projects, most BDA projects are a team effort. Collaboration serves to reinforce the joint understanding of the domain and the types of problems the team is trying to solve.

Big data analytics, with its need for many skill sets, is normally done in multidisciplinary teams. There are multiple organizational structures for locating and managing this team. For example, how are analytics teams set up across the organization, how do they interact with the business units, and how are they compensated? How are projects assigned and tracked? We outline several possible organizational analytics structures in the following text.

Distributed Analytics—Analytics within the Business Unit

In a distributed analytics structure, as depicted in Figure 4.4, analysts sit in one or more business units, and there is no enterprise-wide analytics perspective. This is a typical structure within less mature analytically based organizations. This structure has the advantage that it allows a quick start-up to provide the ability to prioritize, test out, and refine different "pilot" approaches before

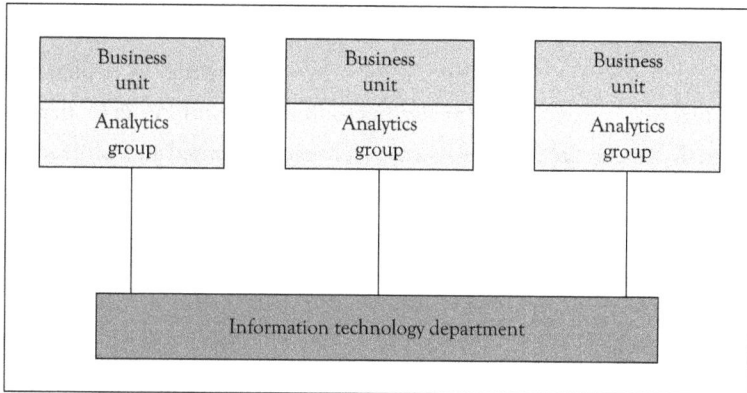

Figure 4.4 Distributed analytics group

implementing them enterprise wide. The disadvantage is that only the business unit with the analytics directly benefits from the efforts.

Centralized Analytics Group

A centralized analytics structure, as depicted in Figure 4.5, is one in which the analytics team is organized as a single centralized unit and sets the analytical direction for the organization. The team can consult to individual business units for analytic services. Analytic services can be deployed strategically. Analytical insights and knowledge across business units can be centralized and shared.

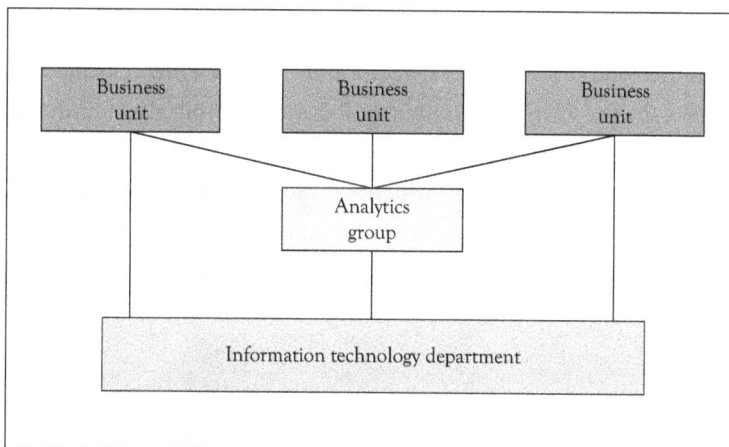

Figure 4.5 Centralized analytics group

Analytics Group within the IT Department

An analytics group within the IT department structure, as depicted in Figure 4.6, is one where the analytics group resides within the IT department. This structure is normally very technology-focused and while it can be very technically advanced, the challenge within this structure is a lack of communication and understanding of the business stakeholders and business needs.

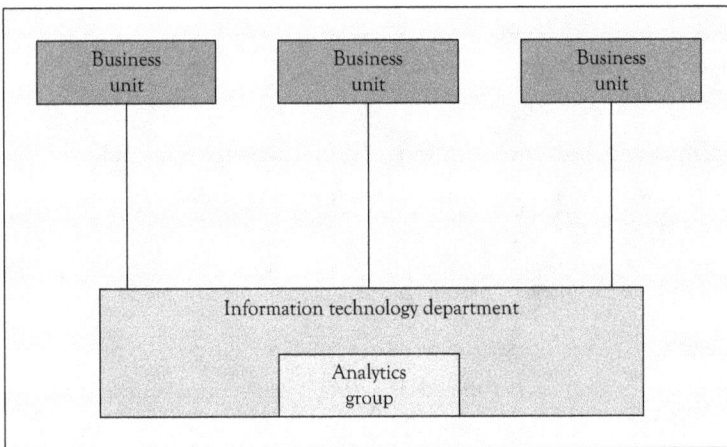

Figure 4.6 Analytics group within the IT department

Distributed Analytics Groups within the IT and Business Units

Another analytics organizational structure having distributed analytics groups within the IT department and business units is depicted in Figure 4.7. The IT-based group can focus on the big data technology challenges, while the business unit focuses on the use and application of analytics. The danger with this approach is that the individual groups may be uncoordinated in these analytic approaches and there is no overall enterprise governance.

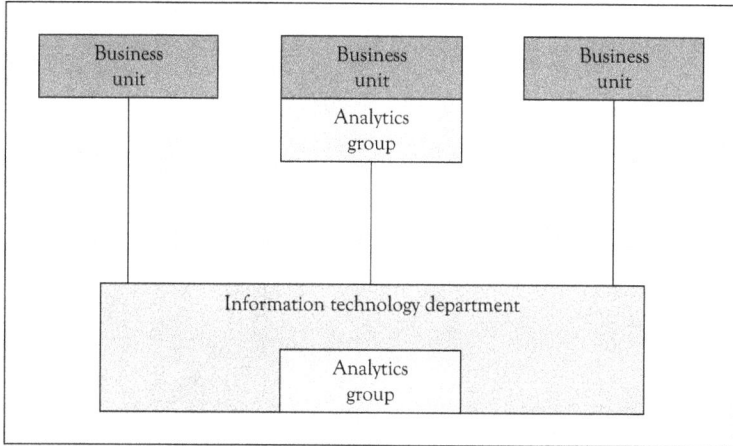

*Figure 4.7 Distributed analytics groups within the IT
and business units*

Methods-Based Analytics Taxonomy

Business analytics has recently focused on statistical analysis, data mining, and statistical machine-learning methods to analyze big data. These are mathematical methods that work with numerical data or symbolic data encoded as numerical data, but they do not capture the domain material that reflects critical factors that affect business decisions, such as culture, political environment, gender, age, and ethnic preferences, geographic and demographic features, and so on.

There are a multitude of other methods for analyzing data and information. Table A.1 presents the taxonomy of analytics based on classes of methods. This taxonomy was first developed by Stephen Kaisler and Claudio Cioffi-Revilla (Kaisler and Cioffi-Revilla 2007). Each class represents many different methods, each with its own advantages and disadvantages.

Table A.1 Taxonomy of analytic classes

Analytic class	Description
Indications and warning (NS)	Assess situations to determine if any event is likely to occur. The goals are to give a probability of occurrence and describe the characteristics of the event. For example, analysis and prediction of rare earth supply chain disruption due to ROC policies.
Dynamical systems (N)	Usually comprised of a set of differential or difference equations of low dimensionality representing known competing forces. A problem is how to handle missing forces. For example, applying sociodynamic principles to patterns of recruitment for terrorism (Choucri et al. 2006).
(Hidden) Markov models (N)	(H)MMs represent the problem space as a set of discrete states, fully linked with associated weights, and an associated set of probabilities. Input data drives the transitions between states. For example, numerous applications for automatic speech recognition (Rabiner 1989).

Table A.1 (*Continued*)

Analytic class	Description
Event data analysis (NS)	Examine an event stream to identify patterns of events leading to particular outcomes. A problem is how to handle missing or exogenous events due to incomplete models. For example, modeling political decisions in the face of uncertain information (Cioffi-Revilla 1998).
Econometric and sociometric models (N)	E and S models are large-scale aggregate models of actors in economic or social contexts. For example, Paul Collier's work on civil war and rebellion and their motivations (Collier and Hoeffler 2000; Collier, Hoeffler, and Soderbom 2001).
Regression models (N)	Regression methods, for example, logistics regression, use recurrence equations to relate past results to future values.
Reduction techniques (N)	Mathematical methods that reduce data dimensionality to identify essential variables, including principle components analysis and singular value decomposition.
Game theory models (NS)	Apply rational decision models to 2- or n-person situations exhibiting both local and strategic interdependence in cooperative or competitive situations. For example, the many applications of the "Tragedy of the Common Good" (Hardin 1968).
Expected utility models (N)	Compute the value of certain outcomes for individual and collective choices, as in the case of Bayesian decision theory. For example, analyzing public lottery contests such as MegaMillions.
Control theory models (N)	Apply (non)linear and optimal control theory principles to modeling interactions among individuals and organizations. For example, the qualitative application of Nisbett's work on cultural differences among different societies (Nisbett 2003).
Survival models (N)	Compute the hazard rate or intensity function of a process to determine its lifetime. For example, reliability models for equipment operation or the spread of rumors among a population.
Evolutionary computation (NS)	Apply evolutionary models, such as genetic algorithms, to determine feasible alternatives.
State transition models (NS)	Model interactions between entities as transitions between discrete states over time. For example, cellular automata and Petri nets.
Graph and mesh models (NS)	Model entities linked through one or more relations. For example, Renfro and Deckro's analysis of influence in the Iranian Government (Renfro and Deckro 2003).
Agent-based simulation (NS)	Apply multi-agent system models to simulate human and social dynamics in complex environments. For example, the STRADS geopolitical simulation systems (Oresky et al. 1990).
Field theory models (NS)	Apply spatial field models of interactions among entities to extend graph analytics and agent-based simulations.
Logic systems (S)	Use of logical formulae and systems to represent and solve qualitative problems, including deductive, abductive, and inductive techniques. For example, the application of constraint solvers to support dynamic taint analysis in program understanding (Zhang 2008).

N = numerical data, S = symbolic data.

References

Anderson, J., and L. Rainie. 2012. "Main Findings: Influence of Big Data in 2020." *Pew Research Center*. http://www.pewinternet.org/2012/07/20/main-findings-influence-of-big-data-in-2020

Barlow, M. 2013. *Real-Time Big Data Analytics: Emerging Architecture*. Sebastopol, CA: O'Reilly Media.

Barth, P., and R. Bean. September 12, 2012. "Who's Really Using Big Data?" *Harvard* Business *Review Blog Network*.

Bean, R. April 17, 2017. "How Companies Say They Are Using Big Data," *Harvard Business Review*.

Borne, K. 2013. Statistical Truiisms in the Age of Big Data. Retrieved December 2013 from, http://www.statisticsviews.com/details/feature/4911381/Statistical-Truisms-in-the-Age-of-Big-Data.html

Boyd, D.F. 1950. "Applying the Group Chart for X and R." *Industrial Quality Control* 7, no. 3, pp. 22–25.

Brodkin, J. 2012. "Bandwidth Explosion: As Internet Use Soars, Can Bottlenecks Be Averted?" *Ars Technica*. http://arstechnica.com/business/2012/05/bandwidth-explosion-as-internet-use-soars-can-bottlenecks-be-averted

Buneman, P., and S.B. Davidson. 2010. *Data Provenance—The Foundation of Quality Data*. Pittsburgh, PA: Software Engineering Institute, Carnegie-Mellon University.

Chakrabarti, D., and C. Faloutsos. 2012. *Graph Mining: Laws, Tools and Case Studies*. San Rafael, CA: Morgan and Claypool Publishers.

Choucri, N., C. Electris, D. Goldsmith, D. Mistree, S.E. Madnick, J.B. Morrison, M.D. Siegel, and M. Sweitzer-Hamilton. January, 2006. "Understanding and Modeling State Stability: Exploiting System Dynamics." *MIT Sloan Research Papers*, CISL Working Paper 2006-02.

Cioffi-Revilla, C. 1998. *Politics and Uncertainty: Theory, Models and Applications*. Cambridge and New York: Cambridge University Press.

Cisco, Inc. 2015a. Cisco Visual Networking Index: Forecast and Methodology 2014-2019 White Paper. http://www.cisco.com/c/en/us/solutions/collateral/service-provider/ip-ngn-ip-next-generation-network/white_paper_c11-481360.html

Cisco. Inc. 2015b. The Zettabyte Era: Trends and Analysis. http://www.cisco.com/c/en/us/solutions/collateral/service-provider/visual-networking-index-vni/VNI_Hyperconnectivity_WP.html

Clifford, S. August 9, 2012. Shopper Alert: Price May Drop for You Alone. *The New York Times.* http://www.nytimes.com/2012/08/10/business/supermarkets-try-customizing-prices-for-shoppers.html

Collier, P., and A. Hoeffler. 2000. "Greed and Grievance in Civil War." *Policy Research Working Paper,* no. 2355. Washington, DC: World Bank.

Collier, P., A. Hoeffler, and M. Soderbom. 2001. "On the Duration of Civil War, Volume 1." *Policy Research Working Paper,* no. 2681. Washington, DC: World Bank.

Cook, D., and L. Holder, eds. 2006. *Mining Graph Data.* New York, NY: John Wiley.

Council on Library and Information Resources (CLIR). 2012. Data Curation. Retrieved November 17, 2013 from, http://www.clir.org/initiatives-partnerships/data-curation

Cruz, J.A., and D.S. Wishart. 2006. "Applications of Machine Learning in Cancer Prediction and Prognosis." *Cancer Informatics* 2, 59–77. http://www.ncbi .nlm.nih.gov/pubmed/19458758

Davenport, T.H. January 2006. "Competing on Analytics." *Harvard Business Review* 84, no. 1, pp. 98–107.

Davenport, T.H. 2007. *Competing on Analytics.* Cambridge, MA: Harvard Business School Publishing Corporation.

Deng, H., G.C. Runger, and E. Tuv. 2012. "Systems Monitoring with Real Time Contrasts." *Journal of Quality Technology* 44, no. 1, pp. 9–27.

Desisto, R.P., D.C. Plummer, and D.M. Smith. 2008. *Tutorial for Understanding the Relationship between Cloud Computing and SaaS.* Stamford, CO: Gartner, G00156152.

Eaton, C., D. Deroos, T. Deutsch, G. Lapis, and P. Zikopoulos. 2012. *Understanding Big Data: Analytics for Enterprise Class Hadoop and Streaming Data.* New York, NY: McGraw Hill.

EMC. Inc. 2014. Managing Storage: Trends, Challenges, and Options (2013–2014). https://education.emc.com/content/_common/docs/articles/Managing_Storage_Trends_Challenges_and_Options_2013_2014.pdf

Feinleb, D. 2012. "Big Data Trends." Retrieved November 10, 2013 from, http:// thebigdatagroup.com

Ferraty, F., and Y. Romain. 2011. *The Oxford Handbook of Functional Data Analysis.* Oxford Handbooks. Oxford, New York: Oxford University Press.

Ford, N. 2006. Polyglot Programming. http://memeagora.blogspot.com/2006 /12/polyglot-programming.html

Fowler, M. 2011. Polyglot Persistence. http://martinfowler.com/bliki/Polyglot-Persistence.html

Gantz, J., and E. Reinsel. 2011. "Extracting Value from Chaos." *IDC's Digital Universe Study, sponsored by EMC.* http://www.emc.com/collateral/analyst-reports/idc-extracting-value-from-chaos-ar.pdf

George, L. 2011. *HBase: The Definitive Guide.* 1st ed. Sebastopol, CA: O'Reilly Media

Gigaspaces. 2018. Big Data Survey. https://www.gigaspaces.com/.../files/product/ BigDataSurvey_Report.pdf (No longer available)

Hardin, G. 1968. "The Tragedy of the Commons." *Science* 162, no. 3859, pp. 1243–1248.

Harris, H.D., S.P. Murphy, and M. Vaisman. 2013. *Analyzing the Analyzers.* Sebastopol, CA: O'Reilly Media.

Harrison, G. 2010. "10 Things You Should Know About NoSQL Databases." *Tech Republic.* http://b2b.cbsimg.net/downloads/Gilbert/dl_10_things_nosql.pdf

Hewitt, E. 2010. *Cassandra: The Definitive Guide.* 1st ed. Sebastopol, CA: O'Reilly Media.

Hilbert, M., and P. Lopez. 2011. "The World's Technological Capacity to Store, Communicate, and Compute Information." *Science* 332, no. 6025, pp. 60–65.

Hilbert, M., and P. Lopez. 2012. "How to Measure the World's Technological Capacity to Communicate, Store and Compute Information, Part I: Results and Scope." *International Journal of Communication* 6, pp. 956–79.

Hill, K. 2012. "How Target Figured Out a Teen Girl Was Pregnant Before Her Father Did." *Forbes.* http://www.forbes.com/sites/kashmirhill/2012/02/16/ how-target-figured-out-a-teen-girl-was-pregnant-before-her-father-did

Hwang, W., G. Runger, and E. Tuv. 2007. "Multivariate Statistical Process Control with Artificial Contrasts." *IIE Transactions* 39, no. 6, pp. 659–69.

IBM. 2019. The Invention of Service Science. https://www.ibm.com/ibm/ history/ibm100/dk/da/icons/servicescience

IDC (International Data Corporation). December, 2012. Big Data in 2020. http:// www.emc.com/leadership/digital-universe/2012iview/big-data-2020.htm

Service Futures. 2019. Four Key Elements of a Service Delivery System. https:// www.servicefutures.com

Jacobs, A. 2009. "Pathologies of Big Data." *Communications of the ACM* 52, no. 8, pp. 36–44.

JASON. 2008. *Data Analysis Challenges.* McLean, VA: The Mitre Corporation, JSR-08-142.

Jirasettapong, P., and N. Rojanarowan. 2011. "A Guideline to Select Control Charts for Multiple Stream Processes Control." *Engineering Journal* 15, no. 3, pp. 1–14.

Johnston, L. 2013. "Defining the 'Big' in Big Data." Retrieved November 5, 2013. http://blogs.loc.gov/digitalpreservation/2012/05/defining-the-big-in-big-data

Kaisler, S. March, 2005. *Software Paradigms.* New York, NY: John Wiley & Sons.

Kaisler, S., and C. Cioffi-Revilla. 2007. *Quantitative and Computational Social Science.* Tutorial Presented at 45th Hawaii International Conference on System Sciences, Wailea, HI.

Kaisler, S., and W. Money. 2010. *Dynamic Service Migration in a Cloud Architecture*. England: ARCS 2010 Workshop, Said Business School, University of Oxford.

Kaisler, S., and W. Money. January 8, 2011. "Service Migration in a Cloud Computing Architecture." *44th Hawaii International Conference on System Sciences*. Poipu, Kauai, HI.

Kaisler, S. 2012. "Advanced Analytics", CATALYST Technical Report, AFRL technical Report (based on work by S. Kaisler and C. Cioffi-Revilla (George Mason University), *Quantitative and Computational Social Sciences Tutorial, 40th Hawaii International Conference on System Sciences*. Waikoloa, HI, 2007.

Kaisler, S., W. Money, and S.J. Cohen. January 4-7, 2012. "A Decision Framework for Cloud Computing." *45th Hawaii International Conference on System Sciences*. Grand Wailea, Maui, HI.

Kaisler, S., F. Armour, A. Espinosa, and W. Money. 2013. "Big Data: Issues and Challenges Moving Forward." *46th Hawaii International Conference on System Sciences*. Maui, HI: IEEE Computer Society.

Kaisler, S., F. Armour, A. Espinosa, and W. Money. 2014. "Advanced Analytics: Issues and Challenges in the Global Environment." *47th Hawaii International Conference on System Sciences*. Hilton Waikoloa, Big Island, HI: IEEE Computer Society.

Kaisler, S., F. Armour, A. Espinosa, and W. Money. 2015. "Introduction to Big Data." *Tutorials presented at 48th Hawaii International Conference on System Sciences*. Poipu, Kauai, HI: IEEE Computer Society.

Laney, D. 2001. "3D Data Management: Controlling Data Volume, Velocity and Variety." Retrieved October 30, 2103 from http://blogs.gartner.com/doug-laney/files/2012/01/ad949-3D-Data-Management-Controlling-Data-Volume-Velocity-and-Variety.pdf

Linthicum, D. 2009. "Defining the Cloud Computing Framework: Refining the Concept." *Cloud Computing Journal.* http://cloudcomputing.sys-con.com/node/811519

Maglio, P.P., and J. Spohrer. 2008. "Fundamentals of Service Science." *Journal of the Academy of Marketing Science* 36, no. 1.

Manyika, J., M. Chui, B. Brown, J. Bughin, R. Dobbs, C. Roxburgh, and A. Hung Byers. May, 2011. "Big data: The Next Frontier for Innovation, Competition, and Productivity." *McKinsey Global Institute.* http://www.mckinsey.com/insights/business_technology/big_data_the_next_frontier_for_innovation

Marr, B. 2015. "Walmart: The Big Data Skills Crisis and Recruiting Analytics Talent." *Forbes Magazine.* http://www.forbes.com/sites/bernardmarr/2015/07/06/walmart-the-big-data-skills-crisis-and-recruiting-analytics-talent/2

McAfee, A., and E. Brynjolfsson. 2012. "Big Data: The Management Revolution." *Harvard Business Review*, Cambridge, MA.

McCulloh, I., M. Webb, J. Graham, K. Carley, and D.B. Horn. 2008. Technical Report 1235 Change Detection in Social Networks. United States Army Research Institute for the Behavioral and Social Sciences. Arlington, VA.

Megahed, F.M., W.H. Woodall, and J.A. Camelio. 2011. "A Review and Perspective on Control Charting with Image Data." *Journal of Quality Technology* 43, no. 2, pp. 83–98.

Mello, P., and T. Grance. 2011. *The NIST Definition of Cloud Computing (Draft), SP800-145*. Gaithersburg, MD: National Institute of Standards and Technology.

Monga, V. 2014. "The Big Mystery: What's Big Data Really Worth?" *Wall Street Journal, October 12.* http://www.wsj.com/articles/whats-all-that-data-worth-1413157156

National Academy of Science. 2013. *Frontiers in Massive Data Analysis*. WA: National Academies Press. Retrieved November 1, 2013 from http://www.nap.edu

Nestler S., J. Levis, B. Klimack, and M. Rappa. 2012. "The Shape of Analytics Certification." *INFORMS OR/MS Today* 39, no. 1. https://www.informs.org/ORMS-Today/Public-Articles/February-Volume-39-Number-1/The-shape-of-analytics-certification

New Vantage Partners, LLC. 2018. Big Data Executive Survey 2018.

Nisbett, R. 2003. *Geography of Thought: How Asians and Westerners Think Differently . . . and Why*. New York, NY: Simon and Schuster.

Nott, C. 2015. "A Meturity Model for Big Data and Analytics", IBM Big Data & Analytics Hub, http://www.ibmbigdatahub.com/blog/maturity-model-big-data-and-analytics

Oestreich, T. and J. Tapadinhas. 2018. *Best Practices for Driving Successful Analytics Governance*, Gartner, G00278625

Oresky, C., A. Clarkson, D.B. Lenat, and S. Kaisler. 1990. "Strategic Automated Discovery System (STRADS)." In *Knowledge Based Simulation: Methodology and Application*, eds. P. Fishwick and D. Modjeski, 223–60. New York: Springer-Verlag.

Pearson, T., and R. Wegener. 2013. Big Data: The Organizational Challenge. Bain & Company, San Francisco.

Peters, B. 2014. "Big Data's Fading Bloom." http://www.forbes.com/sites/bradpeters/2014/02/28/big-datas-fading-bloom/

Pricewaterhouse Coopers, Inc. 2009. "12th Annual Global CEO Survey, Redefining Success." http://www.pwc.ch/user_content/editor/files/publ_corp/pwc_12th_annual_global_ceo_survey_e.pdf

PRNewswire: Dublin. 2014. "The Future of Big Data Analytics—Global Market and Technologies Forecast—2015–2020." Research and Markets. http://www.prnewswire.com/news-releases/the-future-of-big-data-analytics---global-market-and-technologies-forecast---2015-2020-275637471.html

Provost, F., and T. Fawcett. 2103. "Data Science and Its Relationship to Big Data and Data-Driven Decision Making." *Big Data* 1, no. 1, pp. 51–59.

Rabiner, L.R. 1989. "A Tutorial on Hidden Markov Models and Selected Applications in Speech Recognition." *Proceedings of the IEEE* 77, no. 2, pp. 257–86.

Renfro, R.S. II, and R.F. Deckro. 2003. "A Flow Model Social Network Analysis of the Iranian Government." *Military Operations Research* 8, no. 1, pp. 5–16.

Ross, J.W., P. Weill, and D.C. Robertson. 2006. *Enterprise Architecture as Strategy: Creating a Foundation for Business Execution.* Cambridge, MA: Harvard Business School Press.

Satyanarayanan, M., P. Simoens, Y. Xiao, P. Pillai, Z. Chen, K. Ha, W. Hu, and B. Amos. April–June 2015. "Edge Analytics in the Internet of Things." *IEEE Pervasive Computing* 14, no. 2, pp. 24–31.

Shaw, M. 2014. "Big data 2020: What the Future of Analytics Means for the Enterprise." http://www.slideshare.net/hpsoftwaresolutions/big-data-2020 whatthefutureofanalyticsmeansfortheenterprise

Spam Laws. 2014. "Spam Statistics and Facts." http://www.spamlaws.com/spam-stats.html

Taft, D.K. 2014. "Hadoop 2020: The Future of Big Data in the Enterprise." *eWeek*, December 2. http://www.eweek.com/database/slideshows/hadoop-2020-the-future-of-big-data-in-the-enterprise.html

Talburt, J. 2009–2011. "Reference Linking Methods." *Identity Resolution Daily.* Retrieved November 3, 2013 from http://identityresolutiondaily.com/ (Site no longer exists)

Thomas, J.J., and K.A. Cook, eds. 2005. Illuminating the Path—the Research and Development Agenda for Visual Analytics. *IEEE Computer Society Visual Graphics Technical Committee.*

Tiwari, G., and R. Tiwari. 2010. "Bioanalytical Method Validation: An Updated Review." *Pharmaceutical Methods* 1, no. 1, pp. 25–38. http://www.ncbi.nlm.nih.gov/pmc/articles/PMC3658022/

Tsai, C-W., C-F Lai, H-C. Chao, and A.V. Vasilokas. 2015. Big Data Analytics: A Survey, *Journal of Big Data*, 2:21, Springer-Verlag

Turner, D., M. Schroeck, and R. Shockley. 2012. *Analytics: The Real World Use of Big Data.* A Collaborative Research Study by the IBM Institute for Business Value and the Said Business School at the University of Oxford.

Varian, H. January 2009. "Hal Varian on How the Web Challenges Managers." *Mckinsey Quarterly.* http://www.mckinseyquarterly.com/Hal_Varian_on_how_the_Web_challenges_managers_2286

Wegener, R., and V. Sinha. 2013. "The Value of Big Data: How Analytics Differentiates Winners." Bain & Company. http://www.bain.com/publications/articles/the-value-of-big-data.aspx

Weick, K.E. 1995. *Sensemaking in Organizations.* Thousand Oaks, CA: Sage Publications.

Wikipedia. 2013. "Big Data." Retrieved October 24, 2013 from http:// en.wikipedia.org/wiki/Big_data/

Wixom, B., and H. Watson. 2010. "The BI-based Organization." *International Journal of Business Intelligence Research* 1, no. 1, pp. 13–28.

Wong, P.C., and J. Thomas. 2004. "Visual Analytics." *IEEE Computer Graphics and Applications* 24, no. 5, pp. 20–21.

Zhang, H., S.L. Albin, S. Wagner, D.A. Nolet, and S. Gupta. 2010. "Determining Statistical Process Control Baseline Periods in Long Historical Data Streams." *Journal of Quality Technology* 42, no. 1, pp. 21–35.

Zhang, Y. 2008. *Constraint Solver Techniques for Implementing Precise and Scalable Static Program Analysis*. Technical University of Denmark, IMM-PHD-2008-211.

Further Reading

Ayres, I. 2007. *Supercrunchers*. New York, NY: Bantam Books.

Box-Steffensmeier, J.M., and B.S. Jones. 2004. *Event History Modeling*. Cambridge, UK: The Press Syndicate of the University of Cambridge.

Clarkson, A. 1981. *Towards Effective Strategic Analysis*. Boulder, CO: Westview Press.

Davenport, T.H., and J.G. Harris. 2007. *Competing on Analytics: The New Science of Winning*. Cambridge: Harvard Business School Publishing Corporation.

Dunteman, G.H. 1989. *Principal Components Analysis*. Thousand Oaks, CA: Sage Publications.

Forrester, J.W. 1968. *Principles of Systems*. Cambridge, MA: Wright-Allen Press.

Forrester, J.W. 1973. *World Dynamics*. Cambridge, MA: Wright-Allen Press.

Gilbert, N., and K. Troitzsch. 2005. *Simulation for the Social Scientist*. 2nd ed. Buckingham and Philadelphia, PA: Open University Press.

Goldberg, D.E. 1989. *Genetic Algorithms in Search, Optimization and Machine Learning*. Reading, MA: Addison Wesley.

Grabo, C. 2010. *Handbook of Warning Intelligence: Assessing the Threat to National Security*. Lanham, MD: Scarecrow Press.

Hilbe, J.M. 2009. *Logistic Regression Models*. Boca Raton, FL: Chapman and Hall/CRC Press.

Peterson, J.L. 1977. "Petri Nets." *ACM Computing Surveys* 9, no. 3, pp. 223–52.

Philpott, S. 2010. "Advanced Analytics: Unlocking the Power of Insight." http://ibmtelconewsletter.files.wordpress.com/2010/04/advanced-analytics.pdf

Rausand, M., and A. Hoyland. 2004. *System Reliability Theory: Models, Statistical Methods, and Applications*. Hoboken, NJ: John Wiley and Sons.

Resilience Alliance. 2007. "Assessing Resilience in Social-Ecological Systems: A Scientist's Workbook." http://www.resalliance.org/3871.php

Rosvall, M., and C.T. Bergstrom. 2010. "Mapping Change in Large Networks." *PLoS One* 5, no. 1, e8694.

Soares, S., T. Deutsch, S. Hanna, and P. Malik. 2012. Big Data Governance: A Framework to Assess Maturity. *IBM Data Magazine*. Retrieved on February 1, 2014 from, http://ibmdatamag.com/2012/04/big-data-governance-a-framework-to-assess-maturity

Scott, J. 2000. *Social Network Analysis: A Handbook*. London, UK: Sage Publications.

Tufte, E.R. 2001. *The Visual Display of Quantitative Information.* 2nd ed. Cheshire, CT: Graphics Press.

Walter, C. 2005. "Insights: Kryder's Law." *Scientific American.* Retrieved November 3, 2013 from, http://www.scientificamerican.com/article.cfm?id=kryders-law

Webb, J., and T. O'Brien. 2013. Big Data Now. Sebastopol, CA: O'Reilly Media.

Weld, W.E. 1959. *How to Chart: Facts from Figures with Graphs.* Norwood, MA: Codex Book Company, Inc.

Welling, M. 2011. "A First Encounter with Machine Learning." https://www.ics.uci.edu/~welling/teaching/ICS273Afall11/IntroMLBook.pdf

Wills, G. 2012. *Visualizing Time.* New York, NY: Springer-Verlag.

Glossary

Advanced analytic. A set of analytics integrated through an analytic architecture to solve a complex problem.

Analytics. The process of transforming data into insight for the purpose of making decisions.

Analytic architecture. A software architecture or application framework designed to solve a set of problems within a complex domain.

AnBoK. Analytics Body of Knowledge, a compendium of information about different types of analytics.

Application programming interface (API). A set of functions, procedures, or methods implemented in an application, which allows programs to invoke the functionality therein.

Big data. The volume of data just beyond our capacity to process efficiently by traditional database tools and methods.

Business analytics. The application of analytics specifically in the sphere of business, for example, to include marketing analytics, CRM analytics, operations analytics, and so on.

C/C++/C#. A suite of programming languages with low-level features widely used in government, academia, and industry (although waning in favor of Python, Java, and R). C/C++ originated with Bell Labs, but there are many variants. C# is Microsoft's object-oriented implementation of C.

Cloud Computing. a term used to describe an assembly of processors on storage systems interconnected by a network that allows dynamic allocation of resources to meet the needs of different application.

Data mining. A term often used interchangeably with analytics, but, in fact, is a subset of the realm of analytics. Data mining is usually based on statistical methods, but includes variants such as text mining, web mining, and so on.

Geospatial analytics. The integration of geographic and demographic information into the analysis process.

HTML. HypertText Markup language is a specification for describing web pages in a structured way that facilitates their presentation independent of the web browser.

Java. A programming language with a rich library of packages covering many different programming problems.

Java Development Kit (JDK). A software suite comprising a compiler and numerous libraries that facilitate a wide variety of Java applications.

Machine learning. A discipline in which a program is designed in such a way that it can improve its behavior by processing data, examining the results, and deducing or inferring changes to program parameters that result in an improvement in some figure of merit.

Platform. A hardware or software system for performing computations, processing data, storing data and information, and visualizing data and information. An example of a hardware platform is a Dell or Apple laptop or server, while an example of a software platform is Apple's MacOS or Microsoft's Windows 2013 Server operating system.

Population imbalance. The phenomenon whereby in very large data sets, events of interest occur relatively infrequently.

Python. A programming language and system for scripting that is widely used in many environments for fast prototyping of applications.

R. A programming language with a rich library of contributed packages originally developed for the social sciences but applicable to almost any application problem. Maintained by the R Project at www.r-project.com.

RDF. Resource Description Framework is an extension to XML that allows for the enhanced modeling and representation of information using triples in the form subject-predicate-object. It is vendor-neutral and operating system independent.

REST. Representational State Transfer is a service using textual representations and a small API that allows programs on different servers to communicate data reliably and efficiently.

RFID. Radio Frequency Identification Device, a device which responds to specific radio frequencies and returns several bits of digital information.

RTBDA. real-time big data analytics.

Spark. An ecosystem written in the Scala programming language for constructing analytics using resilient, in-memory techniques (faster than MapReduce).

Visual analytics. The science of analytical reasoning facilitated by interactive visual interfaces.

Web service. A method of communication between two computing systems linked through a network, but, typically, a software system supporting machine-to-machine interaction.

XML. Extensible Markup Language is a specification for describing the fields and values of a document in a structured form.

About the Contributors

Stephen H. Kaisler has been a senior scientist and senior software architect with several small technology and consulting firms over the past 10 years, where he has focused on machine learning, big data and advanced analytics, natural language processing, video processing, and enterprise architecture. Previously, he was the director of Systems Architecture and technical advisor to the sergeant at arms of the U.S. Senate. Prior to that position, he served as a science advisor consulting for the Internal Revenue Service, chief scientist for analytics, and a program manager in Strategic Computing in the Defense Advanced Research Projects Agency. Dr. Kaisler has previously published 4 books and over 35 technical papers. He has taught part-time at George Washington University in the Departments of Computer Science and Information System Technology Management for over 35 years, where he is an adjunct professor of engineering.

He is cochair for the Enterprise Architecture minitrack and primary cochair of the Big Data and Analytics minitrack at HICSS.

Stephen H. Kaisler, DSc
SHK and Associates
Principal
Laurel, MD 20723
Skaisler1@comcast.net

Frank Armour is an assistant professor of information technology at the Kogod School of Business, American University and is the faculty program director for the MS in analytics degree program. He received his PhD from the Volgenau School of Engineering at George Mason University. He is also an independent senior IT consultant and has over 25 years of extensive experience in both the practical and academic aspects of applying advanced information technology. He has led initiatives on, and performed research in, business analytics, big data, enterprise architectures, business and requirements analysis, agile system development life cycle (SDLC), and object-oriented development. He is the coauthor of the book *Advanced Use Case Modeling*, Addison-Wesley, and is the author or coauthor of over 30 papers in the information technology discipline. He is primary cochair for the enterprise architecture minitracks at both the HICSS and AMCIS conferences.

Frank J. Armour, PhD
Kogod School of Business
American University
Washington, DC
farmour@american.edu

J. Alberto Espinosa was formerly the chair of the Information Technology Department, a full professor and a Kogod Research Professor at the Kogod School of Business, American University. He holds a PhD and a master's degree in information systems from the Tepper School of Business at Carnegie Mellon University, a master's degree in business administration from Texas Tech University, and a mechanical engineering degree from Pontificia Universidad Catolica. His research focuses on coordination and performance in global technical projects across global boundaries, particularly distance and time separation (e.g., time zones). His work has been published in leading scholarly journals, including *Management Science*, *Organization Science*, *Information Systems Research*, the *Journal of Management Information Systems*, *IEEE Transactions on Software Engineering*, *IEEE Transactions on Engineering Management*, and *Communications of the ACM*.

J. Alberto Espinosa, PhD
Professor and Chair
Kogod School of Business
American University
Washington, DC
alberto@american.edu

William H. Money is an associate professor at the School of Business, The Citadel, Charleston, SC; he joined the Citadel in August 2014. He served as an associate professor of information systems at the George

Washington University and as the director of the Executive Master of Science in Information Systems program. He joined the George Washington University, School of Business and Public Management faculty in September 1992 after acquiring over 12 years of management experience in the design, development, installation, and support of management information systems (1980–1992). His publications over the last six years and recent research interests focus on collaborative solutions to complex business problems; business process engineering and analytics; and information system development, collaboration, and workflow tools and methodologies. His previous teaching experience includes Purdue, Kent State, and American Universities. His academic training includes a PhD in organizational behavior/systems engineering, 1977, Northwestern University, Graduate School of Management; an MBA in management, 1969, Indiana University; and a BA in political science, 1968, University of Richmond. He has had numerous speaking engagements at professional meetings and publishes in information systems and management journals. He has significant consulting experience in private, federal organizations, including the Department of State, D.C. Government, Department of Transportation, Coast Guard, and Department of the Navy.

William H. Money, PhD
Associate Professor
School of Business Administration
The Citadel
Charleston, SC
wmoney@citadel.edu

Index

OTHER TITLES IN OUR SERVICE SYSTEMS AND INNOVATIONS IN BUSINESS AND SOCIETY COLLECTION

Jim Spohrer, IBM and Haluk Demirkan, Arizona State University, *Editors*

- *How Can Digital Technologies Improve Public Services and Governance?* by Nagy K. Hanna
- *The Accelerating TechnOnomic Medium ('ATOM'): It's Time to Upgrade the Economy* by Kartik Gada
- *Sustainability and the City: The Service Approach* by Adi Wolfson
- *How Creating Customer Value Makes You a Great Executive* by Gautam Mahajan
- *Everything Old is New Again: How Entrepreneurs Use Discourse Themes to Reclaim Abandoned Urban Spaces* by Miriam Plavin-Masterman
- *The Interconnected Individual: Seizing Opportunity in the Era of AI, Platforms, Apps, and Global Exchanges* by Hunter Hastings
- *T-Shaped Professionals: Adaptive Innovators* by Yassi Moghaddam, Haluk Demirkan, and James Spohrer
- *Co-Design, Volume I: Practical Ideas for Learning Across Complex Systems* by Mark Gatenby and Stefan Cantore
- *Co-Design, Volume II: Practical Ideas for Designing Across Complex Systems* by Mark Gatenby
- *Co-Design, Volume III: Practical Ideas for Developing Across Complex Systems* by Stefan Cantore
- *The Value Imperative* by Gautam Mahajan
- *Virtual Local Manufacturing Communities: Online Simulations of Future Workshop Systems* by William Sims Bainbridge
- *Service Excellence in Organizations, Volume I: Eight Key Steps to Follow and Achieve It* by Fiona Urquhart
- *Service Excellence in Organizations, Volume II: Eight Key Steps to Follow and Achieve It* by Fiona Urquhart
- *Obtaining Value from Big Data for Service Systems, Second Edition, Volume II: Big Data Technology* by Stephen H. Kaisler, Frank Armour, J. Alberto Espinosa, and William Money

Announcing the Business Expert Press Digital Library

Concise e-books business students need for classroom and research

This book can also be purchased in an e-book collection by your library as

- a one-time purchase,
- that is owned forever,
- allows for simultaneous readers,
- has no restrictions on printing, and
- can be downloaded as PDFs from within the library community.

Our digital library collections are a great solution to beat the rising cost of textbooks. E-books can be loaded into their course management systems or onto students' e-book readers.

The **Business Expert Press** digital libraries are very affordable, with no obligation to buy in future years. For more information, please visit **www.businessexpertpress.com/librarians**.
To set up a trial in the United States, please email **sales@businessexpertpress.com**.

www.ingramcontent.com/pod-product-compliance
Lightning Source LLC
Chambersburg PA
CBHW061331220326
41599CB00026B/5139